Lillian Too's
Easy-to-use
Feng Shui
for Love

*This book is dedicated with love and affection to my daughter,
Jennifer Too.*

*I want to thank my editor, Liz Dean, for transforming my manuscript into this
beautiful book on love. Her selection of images and design is both sympatico and
sensitive. It has helped me make the practice of feng shui easy, accessible and fun,
without losing the essence and nuances of the practice. It has been delightful
working with her and with Collins and Brown. Many thanks, Liz, from my heart.*

Lillian Too's Easy-to-use Feng Shui for Love

C&B

COLLINS & BROWN

First published in Great Britain in 2000
by Collins & Brown Limited
London House
Great Eastern Wharf
Parkgate Road
London SW11 4NQ

Distributed in the United States and Canada by Sterling Publishing Co.,
387 Park Avenue South, New York, NY 10016, USA

1 3 5 7 9 8 6 4 2

British Library Cataloguing-in-Publication Data:
A catalogue record for this title is availble from the British Library.

ISBN 1 85885-758-8 (paperback)
Edited and designed by Collins & Brown Limited

Editorial Director: Liz Dean
Consultant Editor: Mary Lambert
Editor: Amy Corzine

Picture Research: Gabrielle Allen
Design: Jerry Goldie Graphic Design
Artworks: Kate Simunek
Reproduction by Global Colour, Malaysia
Printed by New Interlitho, Italy

You can contact Lillian Too on the internet at her websites:
www.worldoffengshui.com and www.lillian-too.com. For information
on her exclusive range of feng shui jewellery, contact www.lilliantoojewellery.com

Contents

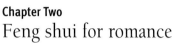

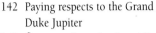

Lunar Calendar Conversion 1924–1995

This is the Lunar Calendar that you will need to use to check your Chinese astrological sign and also to work out your personal KUA number, which is referred to in Tip 68 and many times throughout the book.

YEAR	Lunar Year starts in	YEAR	Lunar Year starts in
1924	Feb 5	1960	Jan 28
1925	Jan 24	1961	Feb 15
1926	Feb 13	1962	Feb 5
1927	Feb 2	1963	Jan 25
1928	Jan 23	1964	Feb 13
1929	Feb 10	1965	Feb 2
1930	Jan 30	1966	Jan 21
1931	Feb 17	1967	Feb 9
1932	Feb 6	1968	Jan 30
1933	Jan 26	1969	Feb 17
1934	Feb 14	1970	Feb 6
1935	Feb 4	1971	Jan 27
1936	Jan 24	1972	Feb 15
1937	Feb 11	1973	Feb 3
1938	Jan 31	1974	Jan 23
1939	Feb 19	1975	Feb 11
1940	Feb 8	1976	Jan 31
1941	Jan 27	1977	Feb 18
1942	Feb 15	1978	Feb 7
1943	Feb 5	1979	Jan 28
1944	Jan 25	1980	Feb 16
1945	Feb 13	1981	Feb 5
1946	Feb 2	1982	Jan 25
1947	Jan 22	1983	Feb 13
1948	Feb 10	1984	Feb 2
1949	Jan 29	1985	Feb 20
1950	Feb 17	1986	Feb 9
1951	Feb 6	1987	Jan 29
1952	Jan 27	1988	Feb 17
1953	Feb 14	1989	Feb 6
1954	Feb 3	1990	Jan 27
1955	Jan 24	1991	Feb 15
1956	Feb 12	1992	Feb 4
1957	Jan 31	1993	Jan 23
1958	Feb 18	1994	Feb 10
1959	Feb 8	1995	Jan 31

A personal note from Lillian Too

My dear Reader,

I hope you enjoy the many techniques which I share with you in this book on Love feng shui. Many of you reading this will feel a mixture of high expectations and good, old-fashioned scepticism. To the former, I wish you love and the luck that brings happiness. The tips inside this book will help you in your quest for happiness. To the sceptics, please enjoy trying some of the easier love enhancing techniques given and allow this authentic Chinese practice to bring you some pleasant suprises.

Whatever your motivation, I want to explain that, in feng shui, it is almost always assumed that love and romance refer to marriage and family. These are attributes of life that are seen as being inextricably bound, and, for this reason, I usually advise young people not to energize their marriage luck using the formula methods of feng shui unless they are ready for a long-term commitment – that is, unless they are ready for marriage and seriously want to settle down. Otherwise, instead of bringing happiness, love feng shui could well bring complications, and even heartbreak.

The taboos and defensive measures described here explain the features you should avoid as well as what you can do to overcome bad orientations. There are always arrangements that can lessen negative or harmful energies. To benefit from this book, I suggest you follow these recommendations and not to wait until something bad happens. Usually when bad luck ripens, it is hard to push back the clock. Therefore, when I strenuously counsel against having mirrors in the bedroom, do bring down or cover mirrors that are present, and do not wait until you have lost your husband or wife to someone else.

And finally, you will see that I have given you extracts of several very powerful feng shui formulas. You may find that formulas recommend different things or offer different analyses. This is quite normal, and feng shui masters always have to decide which formula or method they prefer to follow. For instance, the main door direction is very crucial, and yet you will find different things being recommended by different methods. Flying Star, Eight Mansions and the *I Ching* each offer different suggestions for which corners to energize or ignore. When in doubt, follow the recommendation with which you feel most comfortable. Personally I follow all the different methods but I find the Eight Mansions formula to be the most accurate. It is also the most potent, especially for bringing greater happiness to married couples whose family life is afflicted by bad orientations. I also find the time recommendations of the Flying Star method to be highly invaluable for me in fine-tuning my feng shui. You can do the same.

It is not necessary to overdo things or to be confused. If you read through this book again, you will find patterns of recommendations emerging. You will also then gain a sense of what is important for you.

Welcome then to the wonderful world of feng shui. Take things slowly and let feng shui help make your life happier. Treat it as a hobby. You don't need to allow feng shui consultants into your boudoir. You really can do everything on your own. Doing it yourself is more satisfying and also more meaningful.

I wish you luck and love,

Lillian Too

1

Feng shui for happy relationships

Feng shui addresses one of our most vital needs: happiness, which is not just about wealth, fame, or career success. Feng shui has the potential to transform unhappy lives into happier ones by creating harmony in all relationships. These relationships include those you enjoy with your immediate family – your parents, children and siblings – as well as close friends, colleagues and acquaintances. Most exciting of all is that this ancient technique can help you find a soul mate and life-partner – someone whom you can commit to and, if you wish, start a family. Family happiness is considered to be one of the most important aspirations in feng shui.

Left: You can bring an ideal love or marriage partner into your life by energizing the relevant relationship sectors of your home.

Before you begin, think carefully about what you want from the years ahead. If you would like to meet someone new, think about the relationship you need – remember, feng shui is a powerful tool, so energizing your home to attract a suitor could bring you serious romance rather than a light-hearted liaison.

Using different formulas

There are many feng shui methods for ensuring good family luck (see Tip 2, opposite). Your choice depends as much on personal preference as upon the limitations of the space you have to work with, but feng shui can be just as effectively energized in a studio apartment as in a large mansion.

The feng shui techniques explained in this book represent many different "schools" of feng shui – for some, you need to use your date of birth to find your KUA number, and then your most suitable direction; for others, you need to understand the importance of the eight precious objects – the symbols of love and family luck; and for Flying Star feng shui (see Tips 130–145), door direction and house orientation are the keys to relationship feng shui in the home. Flying Star feng shui uses a system of numbers plotted on a nine-square grid that is imposed over a house plan. Each year, the numbers "fly" to different lucky sectors, so you can fine-tune your feng shui year upon year to get the best from existing relationships, or boost opportunities for new ones. Relationship feng shui brings a great deal of happiness and, when you get it right, you will wonder how you ever managed to live without it!

Love feng shui and the Pa Kua

All the feng shui methods for happy relationships and family luck are contained within this book. You do not have to understand them in detail before you use them – all you need to know are the basic principles, and carefully follow the instructions in the tips. You may notice that there's a recurrence of the number 8, which the Chinese consider an extremely lucky number since it is thought to enhance your luck.

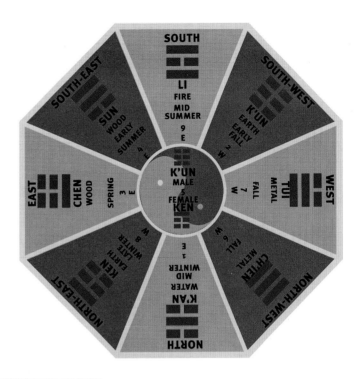

Right: The yang Pa Kua links areas of your home with the five feng shui elements – earth, fire, air, water and metal. There are also associated colour, and life aspirations. The corner of the Pa Kua that we are concerned with in this book is the south-west direction – which is linked with the element of earth and which signifies love and relationships. The symbols on the Pa Kua are trigrams, which form the basis of the *I Ching* and its 64 hexagrams.

Different feng shui methods

Technique	What it involves
Eight Aspirations	Energizing the element of strong earth in the home – this is always in the south-west, which represents love and relationships.
Elemental feng shui	Using colours, numbers and objects in the home to balance chi, or energy. Based on the eight-sided yang Pa Kua (see above).
Feng shui symbolism	Using specific symbols to increase the chance of happiness – the double happiness symbol is one of the most effective.
The Eight Auspicious Objects	Eight objects used to boost love potential. They are: the mystic knot, the cowrie shell, the vase, the good luck jar, the canopy (or umbrella), the sacred wheel, the lotus and the double fish.
Eight Mansions Pa Kua	A person's date of birth is used to decide which parts of their home are lucky for them.
Flying Star feng shui	A system of numbers that relates to a formation of stars known as the sickle. It interprets door directions, and offers exacting perspectives on time aspects of feng shui.

Below: This book uses the yang Pa Kua (above) for analysis of correct feng shui. The Pa Kua below is the yin Pa Kua which is used as a feng shui defensive tool, rather than a tool for analysis.

3

Keep earth sectors strong

In the "destroying cycle" of the five elements, the earth element is destroyed by the wood element. So, in order not to weaken the earth essence in the south-west, it is a good idea to consciously work at reducing the presence of anything that suggests the wood element.

This means that the colours green and brown should be minimized in the south-west. Bear this in mind when selecting curtains, carpets and furniture upholstery for this sector. Also, reduce the presence of metal colours – i.e., white, silver, gold and copper – since the metal element is said to exhaust the earth element. This is because earth produces metal and, metal is said to exhaust earth.

Do not place anything metallic in the south-west like TV monitors, hi-fi sets and computer terminals. Apart from the potential of creating excessive yang energy there, these also belong to the metal element.

Brass and copper decorations are most unsuitable there. In the same way, pieces of heavy wood furniture, which represent big wood, are also not a good idea.

Teakwood, blackwood and rosewood furniture are best kept to a minimum. In fact, in my south-west corner at home, I have no furniture at all save for a small console table that has lacquered legs and a glass top to signify earth energy.

It is also not a good idea to place plants and other decorative foliage in this area. Live plants may look very pretty and do much for the décor of a living room, but, in the south-west area, they can consume the intrinsic energy of the sector, thereby suppressing whatever good energy is being created there.

You may wish to place a tree symbol in the south-west. If so, it is better to display a gem tree, made of decorative semi-precious stones.

Enhancing earth energy

Left: It is not a good idea to feature anything which symbolizes the wood element in the south-west as it destroys the good earth energy. Placing a glass-topped table in this area, however, will help to promote some good earth energy.

Feng shui for fidelity

Marriage feng shui, for those who have found love with someone they care about, ensures that good feelings are nurtured and grown within an environment that is conducive to ever-increasing happiness. Bad feng shui makes many marriages go sour simply because too many hidden poison arrows are in the home and feng shui taboos are inadvertently broken by those who have no knowledge of them.

Infidelity, for instance, is often caused by unfortunate feng shui. For those who are married, it is a good idea to guard against this by ensuring that nothing in the home is set in the wrong place so causing happiness to be spoiled. Often, small corrections can avoid the many problems associated with infidelity. After all, it is easier to adopt a strategy of prevention than cure, as correcting a problem is often more difficult than preventing it from happening.

marriage feng shui. Swimming pools usually cause imbalance and this could lead to sex and love scandals. The effect becomes magnified when the pool sits in a position that causes infidelity or encourages the man of the house to develop a roving eye. Generally this happens when the pool is on the right-hand side of the front door (i.e., standing inside the house and looking out).

If you have a water feature, therefore, irrespective of its compass location, make certain it is not on the right of the main door. Place any large body of water on the left side of the main door (looking outdoors from it). This applies whether the water is inside or outside.

Getting marriage feng shui correct starts with knowing what the taboos are against having good energies in the home. This ensures they are properly taken care of and do not inadvertently become activitated.

Correct water placement

So, from incorrect sleeping directions and bed placement to setting water (pools and ponds) in the wrong place, bad marriage feng shui can whittle away at love and cause great unhappiness. Because of the latter, I almost always discourage young couples from having swimming pools at home. This is because, while water is usually the best element to activate for wealth, it can create havoc with people's

Good water features

Goldfish bowl placed on left

Incorrectly placed water features can cause infidelity. Always ensure that water features are

placed on the left-hand side of the front door (i.e taken from inside looking out).

Here the pond on the left-hand side of the door is correct feng shui.

5

Banish bedroom taboos

If there is to be a happy, loving relationship between partners, it is a good idea to ensure that bed orientations are conducive to a restful sleep.

There are good and bad placements for beds, and, irrespective of sleeping directions, it is important to be aware of some basic sleeping taboos. Therefore, take note of where beds should not be. The four sketches, shown below, indicate four basic bedroom taboos.

Left: Placing your bed in a good position in the bedroom (see below) is essential for good relationship feng shui.

Where to place your bed

The best location for the bed is to have it diagonally opposite the door, placed in such a way that the sleeping direction corresponds to personalized good directions. It is also important to ensure that the entrance to the room is visible from the bed.

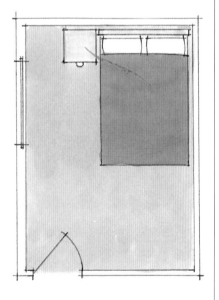

The four taboos

1. Never place the head of the bed directly beside the bedroom door. This affects sleep badly. If the bed is "floating" rather than placed against one wall, the negativity becomes severe. The relationship of a couple sleeping in this position will become destabilized.

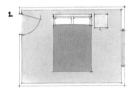

2. Do not let the door seem to cut directly into the bed. If there is another door on the other side of the bed, this problem is made even worse. To solve it, place a divider, such as a screen, between the bed and the door(s).

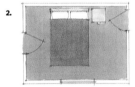

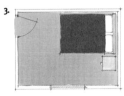

3. Never set a bed across from a room's entrance so that either the head or feet point directly towards it. This creates a situation where one is being hit by excessively aggressive chi. Also, when one's head is pointed directly at the door, it is said to be the "death" placement.

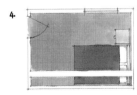

4. Never place a bed directly under an exposed overhead beam, since it causes killing energy to press down on those sleeping below it. Exposed overhead beams can often cause severe problems in a partnership or marriage. Probably the best remedy for this is to install an artificial plaster ceiling which then completely hides the beam from view.

Mirrors crowd marriages

6

Good marriage feng shui flies out of the bedroom door when the marital bed is reflected in a mirror. Mirrors in the bedroom which directly face the bed are the main cause of marriages getting crowded. Generally, they encourage infidelity. In many cases, marriages break under the strain of having outside third parties coming into the marriage relationship.

The larger the mirrors are, the more harmful they can be to a marriage. There are some bedrooms where entire mirror walls create a feeling of space in the sleeping area. These do the most harm. Mirrors on the ceiling which reflect the bed are also bad. Such bedroom mirrors ensure that neither the husband nor the wife will be content with the marriage and will look for satisfaction elsewhere.

The best way of overcoming a problem caused by mirrors is to remove them completely from the bedroom. No matter how beautiful they look, nor now much it has cost to install them, my advice is to remove them.

Above: Placing a mirror opposite the bed is not good feng shui as it can bring about infidelity.

If this is not possible, then at least hide them with a heavy drape, and keep them covered throughout the night. It is vital that people in a partnership do not see themselves reflected in a mirror when they wake up in the morning. Mirrors on any of the three walls that directly reflect the bed (annotated on the diagram below) cause harm to be directed at the sleeping couple.

When the mirror is on the wall behind the bed, it does less harm – but only if it is not directly behind the bed. The acceptable place for mirrors is marked on the diagram.

Mirrors that are part of a dressing table also should not face a bed. If you have no choice, place the dressing table in such a way that its mirror does not directly reflect the bed. Set the mirror against the same wall as the bed headboard, and it will then do considerably less harm.

Where to place bedroom mirrors

Mirrors should not be positioned on the three walls shown if they reflect the bed and the people sleeping there. They can, however, be placed either side of the bed.

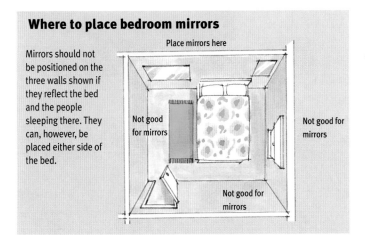

Place mirrors here

Not good for mirrors

Not good for mirrors

Not good for mirrors

7

Bedroom flowers can bring trouble

Right: Flower images on a kimono used in the bedroom are not a problem.

Below: Fresh flowers are not auspicious in the bedroom as they emit excessive yang energy.

Fresh flowers and green plants are best left outside the bedroom. Plants and flowers belong to the wood element and imply yang energy – not advisable for the bedroom. Usually, an excess of yang energy in the bedroom causes problems between lovers, so avoid placing hanging baskets, potted plants and cut flowers in a room used for sleeping and rest.

This is particularly important when the flowers are red or yellow. Red flowers are, in fact, wholly unsuitable for the bedroom and usually spell some kind of loss, so it is inadvisable to send them to anyone who is lying ill in hospital. When the person who occupies the bedroom is sick, they are a portent of death! So when you send flowers to someone who is recuperating from an illness, always make sure they are white or yellow in colour.

Using flower motifs

While fresh flowers may be taboo for the bedroom, curtains and wallpaper with flower motifs are fine. However, do not use over-large flower images as these usually cause relationship problems.

One effect of displaying flowers in a bedroom is that the male of the couple who sleep there will tend to develop a roving eye. This is especially true when

auspicious flowers such as peonies and plum blossoms are prominently displayed.

While these flowers are usually regarded as bringing a great deal of joy and happiness to young, married couples, they make the man develop a taste for younger women if the couple is middle-aged or older. Today, an unfaithful husband is not usually tolerated.

Watch for "evil eyes" in the bedroom

8

Just like mirrors, television screens also have reflective surfaces when they are turned off. Placing a television, or something like it, near a bed produces the same effect as a mirror – and it is made worse by the yang activity of this modern entertainment appliance.

Televisions installed in the bedroom usually cause the separation of the couple using that room. If you find your partner travelling a great deal due to excessive work and career demands, being sent away so often that your relationship becomes strained, then one culprit could be the television in the bedroom. Remove it and this problem should quickly subside.

I was once acquainted with a young couple who had been married for four years. They bought a television and had it installed in their bedroom, directly facing their bed. Far from being romantic, the television caused problems between the couple almost immediately. Whereas before, both had been indulgent of one another's habits and attitudes, now every minor irritation lead to major quarrels and disagreements. Soon thereafter, the husband's job took him abroad more and more frequently. After six months, the wife started seeing someone else and, within a year, the marriage had really broken down and the couple decided to separate.

By the time I came to visit, the wife was on the verge of moving out. I succeeded in persuading her to stay on and work through their differences. But I also advised the removal of the television. I am happy to report that the couple were soon reconciled and are today the happy parents of a baby son.

Another couple who developed similar marriage strains installed a television high up on their bedroom wall. Both had wonderful jobs in the television industry and their television represented an extension of their working life in the bedroom, which caused a schism between them which was so bad that they too wanted to split up. When I insisted they remove it and they did so, their love life improved considerably and they became much happier as a result – and they are still together!

Above:
Televisions, similar to mirrors, are not recommended in the bedroom as they are too yang and can encourage infidelity.

9

Poison arrow shelves

Protruding display and bookshelves create severe killing energy (or shar chi) in the bedroom, which can cause stress and strain on relationships. Especially damaging is when the open shelves directly face the bed, and go all the way from floor level to ceiling.

Open bookshelves are said to resemble knives slicing into the residents of a room, and to cause pain, disagreements and serious quarrels. In extreme cases, exposed bookshelves can create break-up due to gossip and misunderstanding between the couple.

If you have open shelves on any of the walls around your bed, it is best to cover them completely with doors, thereby turning them into cupboards with closed doors. Do not use mirrors for this purpose, as doors that have a mirror surface may reflect the bed and create another severe problem. Glass doors can also be reflective, and there may be lighting in the bedroom that promotes a mirror effect. It is therefore best to avoid glass and to have solid wood doors.

If it is not possible to make doors for shelves, then covering them with a curtain is a second way of dealing with the problem. If you decide upon curtains, it is not necessary to use heavy drapes. Light curtains are sufficient. A third solution is to dismantle the exposed shelves altogether.

Doors with patterns must also be discouraged, since these could well form "crosses and angles" which would send shar chi towards the couple sleeping on the bed. It is for this reason that I am not fond of bedroom furniture that has too many carved patterns on its doors. I prefer it to have simple, clean lines with doors that hide all shelves. Rounded furniture with curved decorative lines is to be preferred over furniture with sharp edges.

Above: Open shelves in the bedroom can cause shar chi, so ideally have cupboard doors to prevent this happening.

Right: Be careful about having any cupboards in the bedroom which have strong patterns as any angles from them could send harmful shar chi across the bed.

Ban computers from the bedroom

Having computer screens and work files in the bedroom causes conficting energies to develop there. Computer screens create problems not unlike those produced by mirrors and television screens due to their similar reflective surface, while the "work" nature of the computer causes distractions that harm the loving and caring side of a relationship.

Keep work out of the bedroom

This affliction becomes more severe when a woman brings work and a computer into the bedroom – an action that directly conflicts with the earth energy of the Kun trigram, which stands for mother earth and also represents the wife or mother in any relationship.

Computers belong to the metal element, and metal will exhaust the earth energy required to nurture and enhance the partnership.

Do not allow work to come between you and your partner. Get rid of everything and anything that brings the office into the bedroom; otherwise, your relationship is sure to cool.

Desktop computers are, of course, more damaging in terms of element clash than portable notebook computers. Also, the latter's screen is closed when out of use, while desktop screens simply become reflective surfaces in the bedroom.

If you live in a bedsitter or studio apartment, and there is not enough room to afford you the luxury of having a private study at home, I suggest that you create a divider that visually separates your bed from your working area. If possible, keep any files out of sight also.

Files that are stacked up and not cleared take on the energies of "mountains" which block the flow of chi in the bedroom. They cause distractions to relationships and should be removed. Storage cupboards in the room will allow you to clear it of excessive clutter.

Remember that a bedroom should be more of a yin than a yang place. It is much better to keep the energies here quiet, calm and conducive to rest.

Below: Work should not be brought into the relaxed atmosphere of a bedroom as it can disrupt a caring relationship.

11 Water taboos and symbols

I often recommend the use of water to enhance one's prosperity luck and the flow of income into households. At the same time, however, I also always warn that the wrong placement of water leads to relationship problems, especially between spouses and lovers.

Water in the wrong place or sector of the house can be the cause of sex scandals, infidelity and marital problems developing into severe and ugly fights. Love really does fly out of the window when a water affliction is serious. This happens when the problem is compounded by element incompatibility and

Above: The water trigram Kan

Below: Swimming pools can be great for children, but be careful of their size as too much water can adversely affect your home.

the effects of bad flying stars. To ensure that you do not allow water to create cracks in your marriage, be careful about swimming pools. These status symbols of the good life represent large water and with them there is always the danger that excessive water energy will affect your home. Remember that the *I Ching* warns against having too much of this and, in fact, the trigram for water – Kan (which is represented by two broken lines and one unbroken one) – is also a warning trigram against having anything in excess (usually material things, such as money). Therefore, pools should always be placed correctly. This also applies to decorative fish ponds, wading pools and other water features.

Placing water features

Here are some guidelines on where water should be placed to ensure that it does not harm relationships and the marriage luck of those who live in a house.

Make sure that there is no water placed in the south-west of your home or its surroundings. This location can bring money luck if the flying stars are good, but having water in the south-west is most inauspicious for relationships, as the water element is in disharmony with the big earth element.

Do not have water symbolism inside a bedroom. In addition to bringing the chi of loss, water in the bedroom causes relationship problems for those occupying it. Thus, pictures of landscapes with waterfalls or paintings of lakes and rivers are best hung elsewhere in the home.

Toilets flush away luck

The placement of toilets in the home can often cause problems, because they are considered to be very draining and represent the flushing away of luck and wealth as water is associated with money. Whatever their location, they always cause a certain amount of bad luck to occur and should never be energized. Yet toilets can cause more harm in some sectors than in others. If you have a toilet that is situated in the south-west corner of your home it is always going to diminish the luck of relationships and family togetherness. This is because water conflicts with the earth energy, exhausting it from that sector, thereby affecting the ability of all the people living in the home to sustain and promote good relationships there.

Right: Toilets are considered negative areas in feng shui and they should not be set against an adjoining bedroom wall or positioned above a bedroom.

Toilets and bedrooms

Toilets can drain your luck when their location is incorrectly aligned with beds and the sleeping direction of their occupants. In today's modern apartments and homes, most master bedrooms have attached toilets and bathrooms, and it is extremely important to note where the bed is positioned in relation to the toilet.

Please also note that, when the bed shares a wall with a toilet, the sleeping orientation of the occupant is very seriously afflicted and, even if this happens to be an auspicious direction under formula feng shui, whatever good luck exists will still be disturbed. To reduce the influence of the toilet on your sleeping feng shui, always keep toilet lids down and the door to the toilet closed.

Toilet taboos

A. The bed should never share a wall with a toilet as this causes extremely bad energy to affect whoever is occupying the bed. Always move the bed to another wall.

B. The bed should not be placed directly under a toilet that is on the floor above it. This causes bad energy to descend onto those who sleep in the bed below.

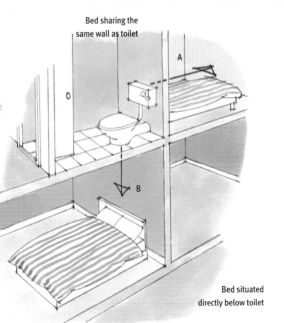

Bed sharing the same wall as toilet

Bed situated directly below toilet

13 Bed placement needs good feng shui

If you want to have good feng shui luck regarding marriage and family, it is important to observe a few simple rules about bed placement that ensure you do not sleep with afflicted energy moving your way. Bad energy causes separations, temper tantrums and intolerance – all of which lead to quarrels and misunderstanding, and when you have this kind of energy coming towards you day after day and night after night, your marriage luck will definitely be eroded. You can use feng shui to reduce this so that the situation does not develop into something serious.

Left: A small windchime can be used to prevent shar chi that comes off sharp corners.

Solving problems

In the sketch here, note the corner protruding pillars, which are sending out bad energy or shar chi, and the entrance door, which is creating bad energy for the bed.

● Firstly, always make sure that there are no protruding corners in the bedroom. These cause poison chi to come off the sharp edges. If these edges point directly at you or your partner, they are thought to create illness and depression, and thereby place a strain upon your relationship. You should either move the bed so that it avoids the line of fire or hang a small crystal or wind chime from the ceiling right in front of the offending edges. Do not use plants to cure this problem in the bedroom. A similar effect is caused by stand-alone square pillars or square tables. If these are in your bedroom, it is important to neutralize their edges in the same way as above.

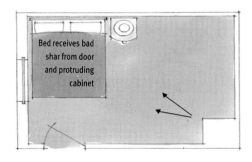

Bed receives bad shar from door and protruding cabinet

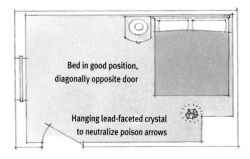

Bed in good position, diagonally opposite door

Hanging lead-faceted crystal to neutralize poison arrows

● Secondly, there should never be excessive fast energy coming towards your bed. This is usually caused by the bed being placed directly in front of the door (see above left). The effect is bad whether your feet or your head point towards the door. It is best to move the bed to another part of the room; otherwise, one partner could well lose the other. This is because sleeping with your head or feet directly pointing towards the door is akin to the death position and is considered to be very inauspicious.

● The best place to put a bed in any room is in the corner diagonally opposite the entrance door. Let the headboard rest solidly against one wall. Select the direction of the sleeping position according to the best directions possible – based on your nien yen direction (See Tip 73).

Neutralize overhead beams

When you have an exposed overhead beam, or a heavy-looking structural ledge against one wall (which has the same effect as an overhead beam), it is important to move your bed out of the way of poisonous chi being sent directly to it. This is because such beams and ledges in the bedroom can and often do create a heavy oppressiveness that can cause, at best, headaches and a stressed mental state, and, at worst, bring about separations in partnerships and marriages.

An overhead beam that cuts across a bed – figuratively dividing it in half – can cause a couple sleeping there to actually physically separate. Even if this does not create physical separation, it will drive a wedge between them, thereby making them grow apart. It is very important, therefore, to cover such beams with a false ceiling or, wherever possible, to dismantle them altogether.

Horizontal beams

Beams that cross a bed horizontally, cutting it into an upper and lower portion, will make the people sleeping there suffer from ailments and health problems. If you cannot cover them with a plaster or fibreboard ceiling, then hanging bamboo sticks or a small wind chime from them will help disperse the bad energy.

The problem with overhead beams is that most are structural and cannot be removed. People sleeping beneath structural beams in multi-level apartment blocks may suffer from severe migraines if they live on the lower levels. Just imagine the same structural beam being repeated on every level of a whole apartment block. In such instances, even using a fake ceiling which covers a beam visually will not completely dissolve the heavy energy created by this.

Decorative beams are less harmful than structural beams. If an entire ceiling is covered with rows of beams, the ensuing pattern dissolves the bad energy.

Thus, in feng shui terms, the most harm is created by the single heavy beam and structural beams. These should always be neutralized.

Below: Sleeping under a large beam can make a couple ill, but rows of decorative beams, as shown here, are thought to be less harmful.

15 Create bedroom harmonics

To give you good feng shui in your partnership or marriage, always protect and look after the arrangement of furniture in bedrooms, especially the master bedroom. One vital component of good feng shui is to guard against excessively overpowering energies in any space. In the bedroom, this means having an overdose of yang energy.

Usually feng shui masters recommend that newly married couples should have their bedrooms arranged in such a way that the precious energy known as yang is created. This is done by hanging lucky red lanterns there and incorporating the double happiness symbol into furniture and decorations. These and other auspicious symbols – especially those that suggest a fruitful consummation of the marriage, leading to children – are believed to augur well for the newly married couple.

Too much bedroom chi

In a couple's later years, however, feng shui masters warn against over-energizing the chi of the bedroom. They suggest that an excess of yang energy causes the man's libido to rise so that he develops a roving eye for younger women, which eventually leads to his looking outside his marriage for sexual satisfaction.

Now, in the past, it was perfectly acceptable in Chinese culture for men in a family to have additional wives and concubines. Often this was done with the approval and blessings of the first wife, whose position as matriarch made her the boss in the household, with jurisdiction over lesser wives. This reflected the pecking order in China's Imperial Palace where the Empress reigned over all the other wives.

In modern times, however, fidelity is usually an essential part of any marriage, so feng shui practice must adapt to modern values and living situations. Therefore, you should guard against the bedroom becoming too energized and prevent the possibility of the man starting an affair for excitement. This can happen if the energies in a bedroom become excessively overpowering.

To avoid this, do not play loud music or place too many yang objects there, particularly the dragon image. The bedroom should be kept quiet, and be more yin than yang. Do not decorate with loud, vibrant colours such as reds, yellows and purples. Stay with cool, soft, restful pastels for a good blend of yin an yang energies.

Top: Lucky red lanterns create yang energy for newly-weds in the bedroom.

Above: The yin and yang symbol represents how their energies interact together. They need to be balanced to create harmony in your romantic life.

Balancing male-female symbols

Feng shui is very much about creating the correct balance of male and female energies in the bedroom as well as the home. This reflects the essence of yin-yang symbolism, which is vital for there to be good feelings in an environment. For harmony, feng shui therefore requires us to focus on this male-female energy balance.

There should not be an excess of female symbols in the home. This happens when its colour scheme and décor appear resoundingly feminine, with excessive use of yin colours – like blues and blacks – and too much yin symbolism.

Balancing yin and yang

Dark-coloured paintings and dim lighting throughout the house are not encouraged. Where rooms are cold, without pets, and there is a complete absence of sound or music, yin energy predominates, and overpowers yang energy. Homes with excessive yin energy suffer acutely from a lack of the male (or yang) force.

If the feminine force dominates a house or apartment, women occupying it wil difficult to have a successful relationsh man. When there is this kind of in between yin and yang in a home, the s of people living there is affected negative they will simply have none. When a h this is occupied by a group of bachelo may find it difficult to meet suitable fe partners. And when it is inhabited k married couple, they will experience fe successes and opportunities. In such place, the feng shui of the environment not right and is unbalanced.

Left: This bedroom has bright, yang energy which is more suitable for younger couples, and less suitable for middle-aged and older couples.

So it is important that master bedrooms are decorated and arranged to reflect a good mixture of yin and yang. Let yin energies prevail, but also introduce yang reds and yellows, as well as bright lights.

For those who are single and wishing to meet someone with whom to settle down, the bedroom should contain yang chi, which attracts the unity of the whole. I strenuously advise my single women readers who are looking for love to hang pictures of men in their homes; and men looking for a life-mate to, similarly, put pictures of women in their homes.

Below: To attract a soul mate, single women should hang some art pictures of men in their homes.

17 Moon yin for marriage luck

Above: For good marriage luck, a girl can place a moon picture in her bedroom.

Below: An ancient tradition is for young girls to throw oranges into water to find a husband.

The Chinese believe that the God of marriage lives in the moon, and there is a charming tradition that is practised by Chinese maidens during the day of the first full moon after the lunar New Year – the fifteenth day of the New Year. At that time, when the moon shines full in all its glory, and when yin chi is at its most powerful, young ladies who wish to find themselves good husbands, and to obtain the blessing of the God of marriage, will throw ripe, succulent oranges into a body of water. It is believed that the winds and the waters will then carry the message across the seas and oceans to bring home an upright and honourable young man for the young lady. The full moon signifies the blessings and assistance of the God of marriage. This custom continues to be practised by very modern young misses in Penang, where I remember having participated in just such a ritual, myself, when a teenager.

Finding a good husband

It is believed that if you want a good husband, you should make sure that the orange fruit that you throw into the sea (or river) is ripe and luscious. Chinese matriarchs go to great pains to ensure that the oranges are sweet and succulent, as this will reflect the wealth and social status of husbands-to-be. Each girl throws just one orange into the sea, for just one chance.

Feng shui in the bedroom is an extension of this belief in the efficacy of the moon. The moon's power supposedly enhances a family's chances of attracting a suitable son-in-law. It is, therefore, a good idea to simulate moon energy in the bedroom if marriage luck is required. One way is to place a picture of scenery with moonlight there.

Sun yang to boost your social life

While moon yin stimulates the luck of marriage, the sun symbol increases yang energy in the home, bringing about a more active social life filled with friendship and relationship oppportunities. If you want your married life to be filled with lots of friends and social activity, you can energize this yang energy. And if you are single and wish to create a fuller and happier social life, then positive yang energy is what you need. You can bring this about this by placing red lights or lanterns in the south-west corner of your home – not in the bedroom but in its social areas like the dining and living rooms. Red or yellow lampshades are wonderful stimulants, since these bring sunshine energy into a house. Better still, have sun symbols incorporated into your decorating scheme. Look for paintings which have scenes that are bathed in sunlight or use a sun symbol.

Above: The sun is a powerful yang symbol and can be used in decoration to help boost your social life.

Below: Light some candles for yang energy in the south-west area of your home.

Energizing crystals

My way of bringing sun energies into my home is to invigorate my decorative crystals regularly. Once a week, I place all of my natural quartz and other display crystals in the sun for at least three to four hours. I like to put them out from around eleven-thirty to about 3 p.m. This ensures that they are bathed and charged with both morning and afternoon sunshine energy. This process of charging crystals is also extremely purifying, since bright sunshine destroys any lingering negative energies which inadvertently may have been stored in them.

Negative energies include anger caused by household disagreements, negative-minded visitors and occasional temper tantrums. The sun's powerful rays will dissolve all such energies and will charge your crystals once again.

Crystals are best placed in the earth corners of your living and dining rooms – the south-west and north-east. The centre of the house is also an auspicious place.

My home has them in these positions and it is always filled with visitors. The phone never stops ringing and my family's social life is also positive and rewarding.

19 Door feng shui for harmony

Whether siblings can get along with goodwill, love and support really depends on their astrological element compatibility. Hence, it is a good idea to have readings of their four pillars charts done, to discover their ruling eight elements. The four pillars chart is, basically, an element road map of an individual's basket of elements; it indicates which element-personality clicks best with him or her. Of course incompatible siblings still must live in the same house together, but it is possible to use feng shui to bring about greater harmony between siblings so that, even if they are not astrologically compatible, they may at least learn how to get along and not to argue all the time. Real respect and support could even grow between them if the feng shui of their respective bedrooms is not in conflict – that is, their room's location in the house in relation to each other.

How to help your children get on

● Do not have more than two of your children's bedrooms opening onto a corridor. When there are too many doors in a hallway, there will be too many "mouths", which can create arguments for the sake of arguing. It is best that large families who need many rooms have the rooms located on separate levels – preferably designed so they do not open onto a single long corridor.

● Make sure that all bedroom doors are equal in size. When doors have different sizes, children with larger doors will develop into bullies, while those with smaller doors will tend to withdraw. Inconsistent door size is also bad feng shui, as it creates imbalance.

● Doors into bedrooms should open inwards, never outwards, since this creates quarrelsome energies. Also, doors into bedrooms are best placed at one end of the room, rather than in the middle.

● Make sure that doors open and shut smoothly if you want your children to get along. Nothing harms their relationship feng shui more than doors which get stuck or do not bolt properly.

This is based on the element of the bedrooms, which in turn is based on the compass setting the room.

Below: The feng shui of your child's room can have a big effect on your child's well-being.

Allocating girls' and boys' rooms

To ensure good relationships between brothers and sisters in the home, the feng shui of each of their bedrooms should be based on the recommendations contained in the yang Pa Kua (see the summary chart below). Here the arrangement of trigrams indicate the best directional locations for each of the children of the household. This approach not only ensures sibling affection and support for each other but also, more importantly, brings all of them good fortune as well. In fact, the placement of all members of the family, including the patriarch and the matriarch should be made according to the yang Pa Kua arrangement.

Locating bedrooms

When there are two children, a son and a daughter, the son should be given the east bedroom, while the daughter should be located in the west bedroom. This ensures that each will benefit from being in the location that enhances their luck. This also ensures that their family luck stays energized.

If there are two sons or two daughters, then the place of the second son or daughter on the chart becomes irrelevant, and only the best locations for the first and third children are used. For example, when there are just two sons, the eldest should occupy the east bedroom while the second son should have a room located in the north-east. When there are just two daughters, the eldest should take the room in the south-east and the second girl the room in the west. If her mother is missing, then she should occupy the south-west room, thereby taking on the role of the matriarch.

Best bedrooms

Above: When children are sharing rooms, try to place the boys in the east and the girls in the west to create sibling and family harmony. If bunk beds are used, as shown here, it is a good idea to use some material to tent the ceiling of the top bunk to prevent the child on the lower bunk having feelings of oppression.

South-west	Mother
West	Third daughter
North-west	Father
North	Second son
North-east	Third son
East	First son
South-east	First daughter
South	Second daughter

If yours is a large family and your children have to share rooms, be sure to always place the boys in the eastern sector of the home – this is the location of the dragon and maximum growth – and always situate the girls in the western sector, which is considered to be a joyous, precious and golden site.

21 Bridge the generation gap

Above: Getting the feng shui right in your home and environment encourages your children to be happy and devoted to you.

Good feng shui always encourages your sons and daughters to be devoted. Indeed, this is a cardinal measure of the good fortune of a family. When this is missing, luck is believed to have been seriously diminished, and nothing brings greater sadness and grief to Chinese parents than when their children openly confront them, which makes them feel upset and ashamed. In modern times, any lack of respect and difference of opinion between parents and children is seen as poor communication and often termed the generation gap.

The three best environments

Feng shui does not guarantee complete obedience from children, but it does create harmonious energies that in turn reduce frictions, misunderstandings and show-downs. The air becomes lighter and happier when the flow of chi is correctly balanced to bring this about. Usually this happens when the house itself enjoys relatively favourable landscape feng shui in that:

- The back of the home is higher than the front of the home. This can be in the form of physical higher ground and contour levels, possibly created by the presence of a taller building behind the house or the presence of a clump of trees that are higher than the roof of the home. So long as the back of the house enjoys "support", things will go smoothly for the household, including its inhabitants' enjoyment of descendants' luck. Children and parents enjoy a good relationship.

- Land on the left side of the house is higher than land on the right (i.e., from the inside looking out). This ensures that the children, especially the sons, of the family become worthy descendants, bringing honour and glory to their parents. When you enjoy good feng shui this way, good luck extends to the next generation.

- When there is water flowing slowly past the home, the children of the family are said to benefit enormously. The two generations will think along the same lines and their ambitions will move in the same direction.

Use lighting and dragons

It is only when the home suffers from several feng shui afflictions such as missing corners, wrong contour levels and other things, that problems occur which show up as major disagreements between parents and children. (In feng shui practice, please note that references to children almost always refer to the sons in the family.) So, to ensure that communication between the generations is always good, do make certain that the home enjoys good chi from its surroundings. If the rear of the home is lower than the front, place a bright light at the back so that you symbolically "lift the energy" and, if land to the left of the house is lower than the right, set a bright light on a tall pole shining upwards, again to "lift the energy" here. Meanwhile, if you place a small dragon image along the eastern wall of your living room it will encourage the sons of the family to be loyal.

Close the doors on arguments

One of the main causes of frequent arguments between members of the family is due to there being too many doors in the home – especially ones that open to the outside. I have seen homes with as many as five doors, with at least two of them clamouring to be recognized as the "main door". I have also been asked many times, "Which one should I consider to be my main door?" by readers who then proceed to describe two or three doors that are regularly used by different members of the family.

Above: For a harmonious family life without many arguments, just use one main entrance door.

This is a situation that leads to there being "too many mouths" – where everyone is talking and no one is listening. What results is a constant battle to be heard, with much arguing and shouting. The situation is compounded when the living and dining rooms have floor-length sliding doors – creating more doors yet again.

When a home has too many doors, the good sheng chi (best type of growth energy) simply does not know how to enter. There is confusion in the flow of energy, and there are also several divergent flows of chi that criss-cross the home, and these are bound to cause disharmony and imbalance. The feng shui gets disturbed, and often yang energy becomes excessive. The relationships between occupants of such a household will be very unsettled.

Choosing the main door

1. Be very clear which door is the main door. Select one which is most liked by everyone in the house to make sure that it is used and, therefore, energized regularly. The door should create good feng shui orientations for the house so that the back is supported by higher ground and the front faces some empty land. More importantly, let the house face a direction that brings good luck according to at least one compass formula you know, preferably the KUA formula (see Tip 68).

2. Close all other doors, leaving only a back door As for the sliding doors, let these stay closed when the main or back doors are opened. Only open these doors when the other principal doors are closed.

3. Keep the doors into bedrooms and other rooms of the home closed rather than open. When there are too many bedrooms opening onto a long corridor, and these rooms are occupied by the children of the family, they will tend to quarrel more. It is better if rooms do not open into a straight, empty corridor. Correct this problem by hanging crystals from the ceilings between the doors of the children's bedrooms and keep the doors closed as much as possible.

23 Mirrors can cause rifts

Mirrors in a home almost always create extremely powerful changes in the flow of chi. They seem to have a special potency that affects the harmony and quality of relationships between members of a family and household, especially the bond between husbands and wives. When mirrors are placed in correct settings, where they reflect auspicious objects and orientations, they bring a great deal of happiness, but when they are set in the wrong places, they cause separations that sometimes become permanent! So mirrors should be handled with great care. We have already noted the grave danger to marriage caused by mirrors that directly reflect the bed in the master bedroom. In all other bedrooms, also, mirrors should not reflect beds, as they can cause rifts in the friendships of those being reflected in their sleep. Social intercourse for these people becomes a source of unhappiness.

Meanwhile, mirrors in other parts of the home also have the potential to cause unhappiness. When a mirror directly reflects the main door, it causes chi to fly out of the house, resulting in there being no luck that can stay and accumulate. Such mirrors cause some of a home's residents to travel frequently, and eventually to leave home. Constant separations occur, and, when astrological times are bad, these separations sadly lead to permenent breaks. These are frequently between husbands and wives where one party travels for work so much, eventually they grow apart.

The effects of mirrors

Separations can also be shown as children leaving home. Even when a mirror does not directly reflect the main door, as long as you can see the door in the mirror, it suggests that children leave home a lot earlier than expected.

Mirrors placed in dark, unused corners can cause similar problems; the best way to counter this is to light them. Also place plants near such mirrors to ensure that the "growth" energy in the home doubles, countering the bad energy that causes residents to separate.

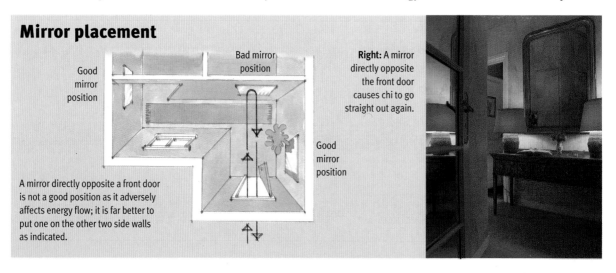

Mirror placement

Good mirror position

Bad mirror position

Good mirror position

A mirror directly opposite a front door is not a good position as it adversely affects energy flow; it is far better to put one on the other two side walls as indicated.

Right: A mirror directly opposite the front door causes chi to go straight out again.

Using feng shui to find romance

It is not only possible, but highly probable that when the relationship and romance corners of your home or bedroom are properly aligned, and correctly activated, your chances of finding happiness will vastly improve.

Also, you can actually be staying in a room where the furniture arrangement or design may be harming your marriage potential, creating obstacles that damage promising and favourable relationships. The result creates havoc with your love life. This can happen if you inadvertently create shar chi, which spoils your chances of finding romance. With married couples or singles who already have an intimate relationship with someone, it can cause quarrels, or bring in a third party. There are several things you can do to activate marriage and romance feng shui in the relevant corner or sector of your room or house. Two methods are recommended: one is based on the Eight Life Situations method, which assigns a specific corner as the universal marriage corner of the home and this has to be activated. The other method, part of the Eight Mansions formula, is based on birthdates and gender that identify personalized marriage direction.

There are also feng shui taboos to be aware of. Bad marriage feng shui makes husbands or wives stray, their sex life becomes bad and communication is non-existent. For singles, bad feng shui can make it difficult to find a partner and relationships break off for no apparent reason. In these situations, feng shui can help those who want to light up their love life.

Attract love chi with crystals

Crystals are very potent enhancers of the earth sectors of any home. Crystals in the south-west promote harmony and love and, moreover, their presence there actually energizes the chi of this area, thereby creating an accumulation of energy which draws love, romance and marriage to its occupants.

To powerfully activate the south-west, consider using a cluster of crystals. For a crystal to affect the chi of a space, it must be fairly large. (Small crystals are better worn than displayed.) Equally effective are solid crystal balls made from crushed natural crystals. Or they can be fashioned into hearts – the universal symbol of love. Always have plenty in the south-west, and light them well to activate them! Always place them on a table – not on the floor.

Look after your stones and discourage anyone from handling them. People's vibrations leave their energy imprints on crystals, and, when negative, the crystals emit negative vibrations. So guard against too much negative energy going into them. For example, when there has been a quarrel near them in the home, do wash them in a salt solution afterwards, and then place in bright sunlight for about three hours.

26 Ignite romance with earth and fire

A quick and easy way to activate good romance luck in your living space is to make clever use of the two elements most often associated with love – the elements earth and fire. These two have a harmonious, compatible relationship, because fire produces earth. Since earth is the more dominant of the two for love, it is excellent that fire ignites and creates earth.

If you want to attract more love opportunities into your life, or perhaps make it more interesting and less boring, you should definitely ignite fire in the south and south-west sectors of your living room. You should use all things red, but also use bright lights.

Red lanterns for luck

A very popular method of igniting romance in the past was to hang a red lantern with the double happiness sign painted on it in gold. This symbol was used even after marriage since it was believed to bring the additional luck of children. Indeed, in the past in China, young newly married couples usually had red lanterns hung in their bedchamber to ensure a fruitful union. In those days, descendants' luck was, of course, far more important.

The influence of fire

Not only does the fire element activate the corner in an auspicious manner, it also represents yang energy, which itself creates tangible forces that are conducive to love. If you want to be more forceful in your feng shui efforts, you may want to consider jump-starting your romance corner by hanging a cluster of firecrackers in your south-west corner. This is, of course, purely symbolic and does not require you to light the crackers. Those of you who cannot find these symbolic firecrackers – used very frequently by the Chinese in the past – to activate this corner for love may wish to use red candles. Place a couple of them in the south or south-west corners of your living room. It is not necessary to light them, although occasionally doing so does give the chi in this area a real boost!

In addition, you should also energize the earth energies in your south-west corner, as this is the important sector that governs the quality and quantity of the romance and marriage luck in your life.

I have discovered that the most powerful energizers for this sector are auspicious objects that are made from semi-precious stones or crystals. These stones originate in the ground and represent the harvest of the earth.

Energize for love only when you are ready for a commitment

You should not attempt to hang the red lantern if you are not ready for a commitment and do not wish to get married yet. In the past, the lighting and display of a red lantern symbolized the happy coupling of two lovers, and it usually signified marriage. It is, therefore, a symbolic activation of marriage luck when placed in the bedroom of a young lady of marriageable age.

If all you want is a more active social life, it is not advisable to use the more serious energizers of marriage. This is because energizing for marriage luck often works in ways which may not be what you really want. If you only want to meet more people and not a mate or partner, it is sufficient to hang lights in the south-west corner.

Feng shui can help to create the chi energy that brings you a mate. It also can attract opportunities for finding love and creating a family. But feng shui cannot guarantee that the union will necessarily be successful. The quality of the person whom you marry, and how long you can be happy with him or her, depends entirely on you and your own karmic luck – and not on feng shui.

I have repeatedly stressed this point many times, and, in the course of the last few years, I am happy to say that I have helped many young people find love and each other. Some of these marriages have been very successful but, alas, not all have had equally happy outcomes.

Right: You can activate your south-west corner to find a partner, but the success of the relationship depends on you.

Too many bedroom doors

Having too many doors to the bedroom can cause disharmony and arguments in a relationship.

The sleeping orientation below brings enormous bad luck.

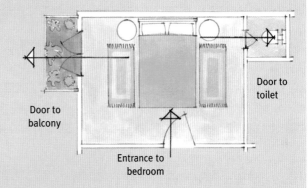

Door to balcony

Door to toilet

Entrance to bedroom

Bedroom feng shui

One young lady, who was desperate to get married, tied the knot with the first man who came into her life after she had energized her south-west corner with the double happiness red lantern. Like her, he too was ready to settle down to start a family, but, unfortunately, what started out with such promise is ending badly. They have separated amidst recriminations. I found it rather sad and went to investigate their marital home, only to find that they were sleeping in a bedroom with three doors. The feng shui of their bedroom was so bad that I believe they never really had a chance. So, even after you get married, do continue to feng shui your bedroom!

28

Boosting your love corner

This technique is based on Eight Life Situations feng shui, where the eight-sided Pa Kua is superimposed onto a room or house. Use a compass to identify the south-west sector. This is the universal marriage, romance and family area. It is necessary to locate this by standing in the middle of the house, because when you are dealing with location rather than direction, taking your bearings from the centre is deemed to be more accurate. To find the love corner in your bedroom, use the same method – stand in the centre of your bedroom and use a compass to identify the south-west corner of the room.

Please note that the method used in this book is an authentic Chinese procedure based on the *I Ching* for identifying the south-west as the love corner. A compass is used to find directions and orientations. It does not use the position of the main door of your home to arbitrarily assign "directions" to each sector of the home.

The south-west sector is deemed to govern marriage, social and love luck because of the trigram assigned to it. This is the powerful trigram Kun, which is the most yin of all the trigrams. Kun symbolizes the powerful chi of the matriarch – the female/ maternal force which governs the family and the emotional well-being of everyone in it. Matriarchal energy nurtures or dismisses love!

Above: A compass can help you work out your bedroom's south-west position.

The south-west should be activated to attract good marriage and romance feng shui. The tools that can be used for activating this corner are many, but if you have a toilet, kitchen or storeroom here, it is best to do something to correct what is an affliction (e.g. by relocating these unsuitable rooms) before you even attempt to activate the corner. For instance, if the south-west is a toilet, and you energize the corner by placing flowers in the toilet, you may attract potential suitors, but they will always be unsuitable!

It is necessary, therefore, to first see what is in the marriage sector before attempting to activate it. Under this method of feng shui, the way to energize the south-west corner of the room is to use objects of the earth element. Symbols associated with earth should be used and the best energizers are natural quartz crystals. Place these on a table with a marble or stone top. You can also hang a painting in the south-west which shows mountains and beautiful scenery to symbolize earth. Keep the area well-lit always, since fire produces earth.

Other fire symbols can also be used quite effectively, here, for example, you can add porcelain figures of horses and snakes here, since these two animals symbolize the fire element, or alternatively you can set a red lantern or lampshade in a corner!

Finding your romance corner

29

There are two recognized feng shui methods for identifying the romance or south-west sector of your home. Either of these two methods is equally acceptable, and both use a compass. When you have successfully found which portion of your home or room represents the south-west, you can then identify this sector as the area for romance luck. This is the area to be energized.

The two procedures are the Pie Chart method and the Lo Shu method.

The Pie Chart method works by superimposing a circular division of a floorplan of your home, based upon compass readings, which is divided from the centre all the way out to the edges of its boundary. The south-west is thus perceived as a "slice" of the whole home area – a pie which is one of eight divisions, with each piece of the pie going from the centre downwards.

The south-west corner

I normally use the Pie Chart method (left) for demarcating the love and romance corner in a home, while, for other compass feng shui formulas, I use the Lo Shu method (below).

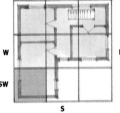

The Lo Shu method superimposes a grid onto the home or room's layout, as shown on the right, and divides it into nine equal grids. The grid which occupies the south-west portion is the part that represents love and romance. It is one of nine sectors of the house, whose center is treated as a separate sector. In the example shown above, the compass reading shows the south-west as the bottom right-hand corner.

Enhancing your social life

30

If you want to use feng shui to enhance your social life rather than to bring you love and marriage, you should avoid energizing the south-west or your bedroom with all of the "heavy" symbols of marriage and family luck. Instead, you can leave your bedroom alone and create a beautiful flow of yang energy in the south-west and south corners of your home.

The south and south-west areas represent the public and social spheres of your life.

Energizing these sectors with symbols will attract lots of new friends and visitors.

So for romance without commitment, rather than display the symbols of conjugal bliss, you can think in terms of beautiful butterflies which signify love that is short-lived. Also, to have plenty of friends of both sexes display a balance of both yin and yang, male and female energies, plus extra yang in the form of sun symbols, bright lights and pets.

31

Checking for feng shui afflictions

Before you start energizing the element energy of the south-west to jazz up your love life or activate your marriage luck, you must look for all the ways that this part of your home may be suffering from what I term a feng shui affliction. This causes the chi there to turn bad, and to send destructive (or killing) energy towards the abstraction it represents, which is love and marriage.

There are different kinds of afflictions, which can be categorized according to the basic fundamentals of feng shui practice.

Left: A very dark room can have too much yin energy and needs to be balanced with some yang in the form of light or bright accent colours.

Poison arrow afflictions

These are caused by the presence of:
● Protruding corners and stand-alone pillars, which should be corrected by setting a plant against the sharp edge of the offending pillar or corner. Another way to overcome this bad feature is to place a five-rod wind chime directly in front of the sharp edge. One may also wrap the pillar with mirrors, to symbolically make the pillar disappear.

● Exposed overhead structural beams and sharp ceiling designs that send killing energy downwards from the top, thereby afflicting the whole corner. Remedy these ceiling afflictions by hanging two small, hollow, copper rods there, set at an angle to each other. The rods should be tied with a red thread to activate their energy.

● Excessive windows in the south-west corner. When there are too many windows in the south-west, love could well fly out of them. Keep half the windows closed or hang curtains over them to ensure that there is at least one solid wall.

Yin/yang afflictions

These can be caused by there being:
● Excessive yang energy, which happens when there is too much light, too much red in the space and too many sunshine symbols. These features are all excellent for stimulating the south-west corner, But, if there are too many, they create killing energy instead. Too much noise can also cause energies to become seriously unbalanced. Yin and yang must stay balanced at all times, so introduce some blues and blacks into the décor.

● Excessive yin energy fills a space that is too silent. When a corner appears to be too dark, and is decorated with colours that are mainly black and blues, energy there becomes stale and stagnant. This must be corrected by a strong interjection of yang energy. Light up the place, paint the walls a bright white and decorate with a dash of red – perhaps in the curtains or in scatter cushions.

Left: A room that is too bright has too much yang energy and should be harmonized with some yin colours.

Remedies for bad or missing south-west corners

If you can't seem to find anyone suitable for yourself, perhaps the south-west corner – hence the marriage/romance area – in your bedroom or house is missing, or maybe the toilet is located there. Or perhaps the elements symbolized by things you have in that corner are clashing badly with that corner's element. All of these problems can be corrected with simple feng shui cures and remedies.

Overcoming the bad effect of toilets

When a toilet occupies the south-west corner of the home, and it is also the one used most frequently, its effect will be that the marriage luck of all the young people of marriageable age who are living in that house will become seriously afflicted. There will be hindrances in their love lives. I have seen many examples of this being the reason that the stunning daughters of my friends just could not get married. When the offending toilets are removed (a hefty job I know!), the obstacles to marriage are also instantly removed. So, try to turn such an offending toilet to some other purpose, if you can afford it. If you cannot, then I suggest that you hang a large, hollow, metallic wind chime in this room in order to weaken the afflicted earth energy of the toilet. Another way to overcome this is to paint the door into the toilet a bright red!

The important thing to remember about activating any corners, including the romance and marriage corner, is that there are two types of symbolic objects that can be used. The first are universally accepted symbols of love, marriage, conjugal bliss, and so forth, while the second depends on element compatibility.

Missing corners

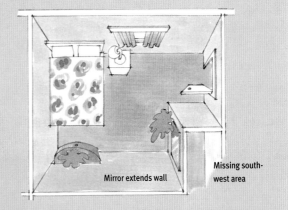

Mirror extends wall

Missing south-west area

If the corner is missing altogether, (as shown in this sketch), you could use mirrors to create an illusion of additional space. This option, however, should be taken only if they can be placed so that they do not reflect your bed, because as mentioned previously mirrors in the bedroom are not advisable.

In this sketch, a plant has been used to shield the wall mirror, which has been installed to extend the wall in the direction of the missing corner.

Use an artificial plant for this purpose if the room is your bedroom, since the yang energy of fresh plants is too strong for this kind of space. Usually a missing corner in a bedroom is caused by the presence of an attached toilet or bathroom, in which case the vital marriage corner has been occupied by a toilet. You will then have to address the more serious problem of having the toilet in your marriage corner.

Some of the universally accepted symbols that can be placed in the marriage corner to attract that man/woman into your life are a pair of mandarin ducks or lovebirds. Using symbolism correctly in your practice of feng shui can often work wonders. So, if you feel like energizing the south-west, look for ducks and birds that are made of semi-precious stones that suggest the vital earth element. This enhances the south-west. Wooden objects are therefore not so suitable.

33 Strengthen earth energy in the south-west

If you want to seriously enhance the relationship luck of any home, whether it be relationships between each other or with outsiders, it is vital that you possess a really strong south-west corner in your home. This sector affects the luck of the mother of the family, as well as the household's general well-being regarding domestic life. If it is missing, it is a good idea to invest some money in order to create proper yang energy in the corner. Do this by building a room there, if space is available, or shine a bright light in the missing corner to set yang energy flowing.

Using element principles

The most efficient way of enhancing the chi of the south-west is to apply element principles in a clever and balanced way. Since we know the south-west is the place of Big Earth, we should create a "small mountain" in that part of the garden. Do this by building a tiny rockery made of decorative stones. This should be only a small mound, perhaps no more than a couple of feet high. Then, to make it even more auspicious, spray a few of the rocks with gold paint. This transforms it into a mountain of gold. Don't add too much gold, since an excessive amount will simply exhaust the earth energy. The idea is to strengthen, not weaken, earth energy here.

If you do not have a garden, use the same reasoning to place a picture or painting of a beautiful mountain in your home's south-west corner. Try to find one that does not have water features. Earth energy is needed, not water energy, so do not hang paintings that have

Above: To boost the chi in your south-west area, hang a picture of a mountain as a symbol of Big Earth or place pebbles (see below) in an auspicious place.

waterfalls, lakes and rivers alongside mountains. I am personally extremely fond of displaying any one of the mystical mountains of the world – mountains that are said to be the chakras of the earth. My absolute favourites are the Himalayas with their majestic peaks, within and especially Mount Kailash – the magical mountain of Tibet said to be the abode of the Gods and the world's heart chakra. A picture of Mount Kailash will surely send strong energy to your south-west. Other strong mountains are Ayers Rock in Australia (shown above) and Table Mountain in Cape Town, South Africa.

To strengthen the south-west even further, place a bright light there. It signifies fire, which produces earth in the cycle of elements. Having a strong light in the south-west is always an excellent way of activating marriage luck. If you want to intensify this luck, you can hang a red light there. Red lights are associated with marriage.

Energize earth with crystals

When you activate the earth energies of your home, please note that you will also be making good progress in improving the feng shui of your home. In addition to enhancing your relationships, other benefits also will accrue. The luck of the earth is extremely powerful, as it supplements your "heaven luck" as well as your very own "mankind luck". When your house has solid earth luck, the whole family stays grounded and there is a strong sense of solidarity. Its members will stay united and will watch out for one another.

How can you energize earth luck?

The best way is to keep the entire home well lighted. Not only the south-west corner benefits from a good dose of yang brightness – the entire house does. Therefore, make certain there are no dark corners in your home. Even storerooms and garages should be happy, well-lit places. Lights bring forth yang chi, which generates life, progress, growth and success, and represent the fire essence, which creates the earth essence.

In addition to lights, you can also use natural quartz crystals to energize your home, especially the living room. I am a great believer in the efficacy of natural crystals, but they should possess clean, crisp energy. Do not, and I stress, do not, display crystals that look sad and defeated – ones with no brilliance or shine – which do not reflect the surrounding good luck. Such crystals bring

stagnant and stale chi into your home. To guard against this, soak all freshly acquired crystals in a solution of water and sea salt for seven days and seven nights. Then, energize them by placing them in strong sunlight for many hours. Sunlight invigorates crystals, and when you place such crystals in your home, they radiate wonderful, positive energy.

Please note that I am talking about natural crystals and you should have your own personal preferences – for example, quartzes, amethysts, citrines, or tourmalines. It is a good idea to place seven types of crystals in your living room, especially in the south-west corner. This will exert strong chi to attract partners to single people in the household.

A third group of earth energizers are beautiful decorative objects made of porcelain or clay. These are excellent for creating strong earth chi. Vases and urns are especially powerful, and they can also be made into feng shui wealth vases.

Below: Natural quartz crystals contain powerful energy that can be used to boost the energy in your living room.

35

Create generations with the Chinese matriarch

The eight trigrams that form the basis of the 64 hexagrams of the *Book of Changes* – the *I Ching* – are the base upon which much of feng shui practice is built. So, the trigram Kun, which is made up of three broken lines, and also represents the ultimate yin essence, symbolizes the intangible force behind the family. Kun is, therefore, symbolic of matriarchal energy. This essence is what creates the family, so Kun also symbolizes the ripening of relationship and marriage destiny, also referred to as marriage karma.

It is this symbolism that makes the south-west especially important for those who wish to create feng shui that will ripen their love, romance and marriage karma more quickly. The south-west sector is the place of Kun, according to the arrangement of trigrams around the compass, and also in the Yang Pa Kua, also referred to as the Later Heaven Arrangement Pa Kua.

Activating the Kun trigram

There are different ways of activating the Kun trigram, which consists of three broken lines. The easiest method is simply to incorporate the trigram itself onto ceiling design, furniture motifs, and other decorative patterns displayed in the south-west sector.

Another method of activating the trigram, and one I favour, is displaying a matriarchal image. This can be a picture of a queen, a female ancestor or any older lady dressed in regal finery. You may wish to hang a picture of the Queen or First Lady in the south-west to symbolize the matriarchal presence. An image does not have to be Chinese in origin for it to create the symbolism aimed for.

Those who want Chinese paintings may find them in the Chinese district of major cities. I have found some in the antique shops of Hollywood Road in Hong Kong. Here there are many wonderful paintings of matriarchs and patriarchs, and these would be an ideal way of energizing this corner. Hang pictures of both the patriarch and matriarch, as this creates the symbolic vigour of the family essence.

Above and right:
Hanging Chinese paintings of matriarchs activates the Kun trigram and brings good family relationships. The queen of the West is shown right.

Decorate with lucky jars

Next, consider vases and urns. The most ideal shape is that of the gourd, in which a small, narrow neck connects two rounded halves (below). Another good shape is a vase with a long, narrow neck and a large base (see left).

Asupicious jars

It is also a good idea to display porcelain jars that have auspicious symbols on them. Therefore, a vase with the dragon and phoenix image would be ideal for suggesting marriage luck, since it is one of the most popular Chinese symbols used for this happy occasion. It is entirely up to you what kind of porcelain you display, and which symbols you combine. I have many urns of different shapes in the south-west area of my home. I keep some of them empty, rather than filling them with water. But I do fill the smaller ones with semi-precious stones in order to strengthen the area's earth energy. I also fill some of the long-stemmed vases with peonies, whenever I can find them, because they symbolize conjugal happiness.

A great way to create happy family chi – whether or not you are already married – is to display the beautiful vases, urns and jars that are so popular with the Chinese. These bring love and happiness to a household, and may be purchased from any Chinese super-market, so that they need not be too costly. Usually, only signature or genuine antique pieces, which have been perfectly fired or bear a rare colouring, are expensive. For feng shui purposes, any reproduction piece in red or yellow is suitable. Yellow is superb for the south-west sector – a colour termed "chicken shit yellow" because it is said to resemble the droppings of chickens. The recommended red is a dark one – almost maroon – which is referred to as "ox blood red". These colours are very suitable for the south-west.

Above: Vases with thin necks and bulging bottoms, such as the gourd shape, are said to keep in wealth.

Right: A porcelain vase depicting love birds will encourage good marriage luck.

37 Sunshine super-crystals

One of the nicest ways of energizing the south-west, and any other area of the home, is to literally bring the sunshine in. This is not always possible as it depends on whether you have a window with a sun-facing aspect. If you do, then you should hang a few one to two-inch-wide faceted crystal balls along the windows. These are lead crystals, and the best are those made for chandeliers. Go to your nearest lighting shop and ask for a few faceted crystal balls.

When the sunshine catches the facets of the crystal, it breaks the white sunlight into the colours of the light spectrum, thereby instantly creating and sending beautiful rainbows into the home. Usually, depending on how large the crystal balls are, these rainbow lights are extremely brilliant, and large as well.

I place these crystal balls all round my home so that, in the mornings, I create rainbows in my east-facing living room and, in the afternoons, the rainbows appear via my western-oriented windows. My south-west corner gets rainbows both morning and afternoon, and this brings a great deal of excellent matriarchal energy into my house. Not only does this add to my and my husband's marriage luck, but rainbows also bring a lot of auspicious luck for me since I am the matriarch of my household.

Rainbows also create precious yang energies that circulate and accumulate throughout the home, thereby vastly improving the chi inside it. Usually, homes awash with sunshine and rainbows are happy homes. There will not be any lack of friends or socializing opportunities for their inhabitants. The great thing about this tip is that it is impossible to overdo since the rainbow colours created never overwhelm a home.

Above: To enhance south-west energy, hang faceted crystal balls in the windows of this area.
Right: Place six smooth crystal balls in the south-west for family harmony.

Bring in opportunities with a phoenix

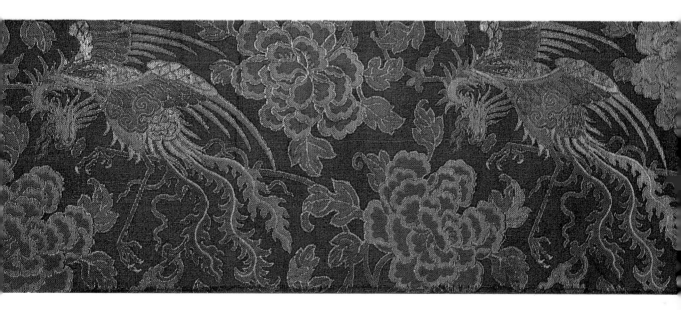

In feng shui symbolism, birds feature prominently in the creation of romance and marriage chi. Mandarin ducks, geese and swans all belong to the family of feathered creatures – and, in this domain, the celestial phoenix reigns supreme.

The phoenix is one of the four celestial creatures of Chinese mythology and is widely regarded as the female yin mate of the celestial dragon who symbolizes the male yang essence. When the phoenix and dragon are displayed together, they signify a fruitful marriage, and this image is very popular at Chinese weddings.

When displayed on its own, the phoenix is no less powerful. Its beautiful presence is said to signify portents of new opportunities. In terms of directions, the phoenix symbolizes the south – with the yang trigram, Li, which also signifies fire. The colour of the phoenix is the yang red. The phoenix can thus be placed in the earth element sector of the south-west, since the elements will be in harmony and balance.

Fire produces and strengthens the earth element, as a result of which the phoenix magnifies chances for love and romance. The probability of finding a soul mate is heightened and the probability of love leading to marriage is also considerably enhanced.

The phoenix symbol

For those of you who wish to place the phoenix image in the south-west, I suggest you look for some of the stunning embroidery that has been coming out of China in recent years, or you can look for the symbol in beautiful porcelain and paintings. You can display the phoenix alone or with a dragon. This is entirely a matter of personal choice. If, for some reason, you are unable to find the phoenix image, you can also use the colourful peacock as a suitable substitute. These have fine and colourful plumage, and they are worthy alternatives to the phoenix.

Above: Place a wall hanging of a phoenix or peacock in your relationship area to bring about romance.

39 Attract blissful love with paired birds

Those who wish to energize the love sector – i.e., the south-west – with mandarin ducks should hang a painting of, or try to obtain, decorative ducks. The best and most powerful energizers are ducks made of semi-precious stones – in transparent or rose quartz, jasper, aventurine, tourmaline and red coral. Made of earth element materials, they imbue decorative objects with powerful earth energy.

Ducks made of wood are less suitable as energizers, since wood clashes with earth, but when they are painted in colourful hues (especially red), they are acceptable, although they will not be as potent as those made from semi-precious stones and crystals. However, painted wooden ducks are better than not having any at all if you wish to create the symbolism of romance, but do not use unpainted wooden mandarin ducks. Brown wood is big wood, and clashes with the south-west earth element.

Mandarin ducks signify the happiness of conjugal bliss, and Chinese artists have always painted these beautiful water birds to signify the love that exists between married partners and between young lovers. When you hang a painting of these creatures in your bedroom, they signify the happiness of two people having found each other. They are therefore regarded as most auspicious symbols for newly joined couples.

Single men and women also benefit from the symbolism of mandarin ducks if their picture is hung prominently in any part of the house. However, having them in the south-west corner of the living room multiplies and strengthens the creation of love energy.

Above: If you can't find mandarin ducks, display a picture of doves in the south-west of the living room to boost the love energy in that area.

Placing mandarin ducks

When displaying mandarin ducks, place them at coffee table level. Do not display one single duck, since this represents a duck without its mate. Also, do not show three ducks, as this suggests there will be problems with your love life getting a bit crowded! Remember three's a crowd. Always display a pair of mandarin ducks – nothing more and nothing less.

Mandarin ducks are excellent objects to have around when you have a family. To create the luck of togetherness, thereby ensuring that the family stays together, you can create a whole family of ducks swimming on a mirror surface. This symbolizes that the family will not separate and will always stay united.

Flying geese for marital fidelity

A pair of geese soaring high in the sky together is one of the most potent symbols of the happy togetherness of a couple. Mandarin ducks are more suitable for those aspiring towards marriage or looking to enter into a relationship with a suitable mate, but those already in a relationship should think of displaying a pair of geese.

A pair of geese extends the promise of two people being gloriously happy together with no separation between them. If you are in a new relationship, and work tends to keep you separated, look for a screen with a pair of flying geese painted on it, or images of two flying geese, to put on the south-west wall of your living room. They make for happy relationships. These creatures have beautiful plumage and are said to pine for their mates. They are said to be so attached to each other that one will never fly without the other.

Geese also symbolize male yang energy, so they are also emblems of good fortune. In the winter, they instinctively fly towards warmth. Being migratory, geese signify the spirit of adventure. They never fly alone, but always in pairs. As a marriage or betrothal gift, they symbolize the wish of togetherness for a couple. Geese are faithful creatures. They do not mate a second time. Due to this, they symbolize undying love. Those who stay true to the memory of their departed loved ones are said to personify the spirit of geese.

Above: Paired geese displayed on a plate, screens or paintings in the south-west living area will encourage a loving and enduring relationship for couples.

Love birds to enhance romance

Other birds that can take the place of mandarin ducks and geese are budgerigars or lovebirds. Some people refer to these parakeets as miniature parrots. They are called lovebirds because of their extreme attachment to their mates. These birds are rarely seen sitting alone. They move in pairs. If you are unable to locate the above-mentioned Chinese symbols, these western lovebirds are excellent substitutes.

Whatever type of bird you use, please remember never to display them alone or separated from their mate. And do not have more than two. If you do, you are only setting yourself up for heartbreak. Keep them in the south-west, either in your living area or bedroom, and keep them well lit.

41

The power of the double-happiness symbol

This is one of the most popular symbols used by the Chinese. It denotes the occurrence of many joyous occasions. Basically, in Chinese tradition, life's three main happiness occasions (hei see) are celebrations of important birthdays, the successful marriages of sons and daughters, and the births of sons and grandsons. Of these three that also qualify as double-happiness events, two concern family or relationship happiness, marriage and having children. The third regards longevity. The Chinese do not celebrate the birthdays of young people and, indeed, seldom encourage it, since this is like tempting the gods. They believe that, unless you have reached at least your 59th birthday, celebrating birthdays merely attracts the jealousy of the Gods.

These "happiness" events are seen as the manifestation of good fortune, and the double-happiness symbol is said to ensure many such events for the family. This translates into good relationships or marriages for the young sons and daughters of the family, and also ensures that these marriages are fruitful, that is, that the family is blessed with plenty of healthy children, especially sons. Indeed, the Chinese euphemism for extreme good fortune is when a patriarch has five sons. When someone wishes you to have five sons, it is like saying, "May you have plenty of happiness".

A strong symbol

The double-happiness sign is, therefore, a very powerful symbol for attracting serious marriage/relationship luck and also, after marriage, for ensuring continued happiness (for the Chinese, this means being blessed with many children) – hence, double-happiness. It is for this reason that I have designed an entire range of jewellery around this double-happiness symbol, which can be worn to attract the luck of extreme joy and happiness. Wear double-happiness rings and earrings if you want to activate the luck of marriage and love. If you prefer to play it safe, and want to ensure that your bedrooms are also similarly energized, then do place the double-happiness sign there as well. Hang a lantern with the symbol or place the symbol in the south-west of your bedroom.

Double-happiness symbolism
Wearing jewellery that bears the double-happiness symbol can help bring joy into your life.

Red and yellow lights for an active social life

If you want to have a more active social life and kindle the embers of romance, go shopping for bright red and yellow lampshades to place in the south-west corners of your home or living room. These happy-looking lights will infuse the corners with a dash of yang energy. Red also represents fire, which produces the vital earth element, while yellow lampshades are said to be the colour of earth itself. Yellow is, of course, also very yang and is a most auspicious colour to use just on its own.

Using red lights

Do not overdo things by placing too much red in the south-west. If you have a red lampshade, it is unnecessary to have red lights or a red lantern, although you could have a red lampshade in your living room and a red lantern in your bedroom.

You should not place your red lampshade too low on a coffee table. It should be at least at sideboard level so that its red light energy is raised. It can also be placed in this position as a standing lamp.

A variation of the red lampshade is to have modern plastic lighting. Little red lights are most suitable for opening up yang energy. Do not place these red lights anywhere but the south, south-west or north-east. They are potent little energizers, but are not good for the west or the north-west.

Red lights should be used with some care in bedrooms as they are so powerful that they can create too much energy. Make certain you do not over-energize them by having too much red on display.

Above: Red and yellow lights are very yang and will promote romance or a good social life when placed in the south-west corners of your home.

43

The colour red – check if it's good for you

When you have an important date with someone you fancy, wearing a red outfit will energize your personality with strong yang chi. The vibrations sent out are extremely positive and can be very romantic. Simply remember not to overdo the intensity and quantity of red. It is especially good to wear red during the winter and autumn months, since the heat associated with the colour adds yang balance to the yin winter months. This same analogy holds true for those whose birth years are ruled by the wood element. So, if you discover that your element is wood and you were born in the winter months, then wearing red will strengthen you considerably, since red brings you some much-needed warmth.

Red is also the colour of things ready for harvest. It symbolizes the ripening fruit of summer and, when applied to a flowering relationship, it is the catalyst which leads to the blossoming of love.

Above: Wearing red can energize your personality for a date, but first check your elements below.

Your year of birth

Please note that everyone has two ruling elements in their year of birth. The first is the element of your earthly branch and is known as the animal sign under which you were born. The second is the element of the heavenly stem of the year of your birth, and for this you will need to check the Chinese lunar calendar. In the table below I have given two categories for you to check your elements. I have indicated all the animals whose intrinsic element falls under each of the five elements. Check your elements under your year of birth as well as your animal sign. So if you were born in 1966, fire is your year element. The first is the heavenly stem element and the second is the earthly branch. Red will enhance romance for both the stem and also the branch that signifies the fire element. So if you are a snake born in 1977 you already have too much fire and should not wear much red.

Checking your elements

WOOD	FIRE	EARTH	METAL	WATER
		YEARS:		
1934, 35, 44, 45, 54, 55, 64, 65, 74, 75, 84, 85, 94, 95	1936, 37, 46, 47, 56, 57, 66, 67, 76, 77, 86, 87, 97, 98	1938, 39, 48, 49, 58, 59, 68, 69, 78, 79, 88, 89, 98, 99	1940, 41, 50, 51, 60, 61, 70, 71, 80, 81, 90, 91, 2000, 01	1942, 43, 52, 53, 62, 63, 72, 73, 82, 83, 92, 93
		ANIMALS:		
Tiger and Rabbit (intrinsic element)	Snake and Horse (intrinsic element)	Dog, Ox, Dragon and Sheep (intrinsic element)	Monkey and Rooster (intrinsic element)	Pig and Rat (intrinsic element)
Great to wear red in the winter months.	Red is great all year round, but in the summer could be too much fire.	Red is wonderful all through the year, but is especially good in the winter.	Red is not suitable at any time of the year – it is better to go for white and yellow.	Red clashes with water, but in small quantities is excellent in the winter.

Jump-start love chi with a red wall!

If you are really desperate for a relationship and want to do something drastic, try painting your south-west wall a bright red. This creates very loud yang energy which fires the chi in that area. Red has powerfully potent energies and, placed in the correct south-west corner of your home, can intensify love chi.

If you have tried everything on a small scale, as recommended, and you are still not getting very far with finding someone you like enough to consider seriously, or you simply have exhausted all avenues to persuading your lover to get married, paint your south-west wall a bright red.

You can paint either the inside or outside of your wall, and you can also use a red wallpaper. Once the red wall has done its job, however, repaint the wall back to white again! Remember that too much red can cause an overdose of yang energy, and there will be circumstances and periods of the year when this can be explosive. So you will want to be a little circumspect when implementing this tip.

Red to bring about marriage

Having said this, I have seen entire rooms decorated in red, and they do look rather stately when done properly. I once had a friend, a crusty, middle-aged stockbroker, who was single and lived for many years in splendid isolation on the Peak in Hong Kong. John was the nearest thing to a confirmed bachelor and all he had for company was an old housekeeper. However, he never lacked female company and, over the years, had honed the avoidance of commitment to a fine art. He was extraordinarily good at slipping through the fingers of lady companions. Poor John lived under the delusion they wanted to marry him for his money. And then he met June Mei, an interior decorator who, after dating him a mere three months, convinced him to have his penthouse redecorated. Mei stripped his walls of the boring dark blues and pasted stylish-looking red and maroon shades of wallpaper. In his south-west corner, she also placed a red lampshade. Needless to say, by the following Christmas, she had succeeded in installing herself as his wife!

Below: Painting the south-west walls red can really enhance the area and increase your chances of a relationship or commitment from a lover.

45 Candles make wonderful energizers

Candles make wonderful energizers for romance. Use red and yellow candles to accentuate the chi of the south-west. Do not use white or black ones, since the chi that emanates from them clashes with the energies of the earth sector. It is not necessary to light the candles every day – once a week is sufficient, or during full moon nights.

Below: Place some red or yellow floating candles in a bowl of water outside once a week or on full moon nights to boost romance opportunities.

On those evenings, you might wish to place several floating candles in a bowl of water. Inside the bowl, place seven types of semi-precious stones. If you have it, set a small piece of imitation gold in the basket of elements you are creating. Adding the gold will make your family luck more complete and auspicious. The last ingredient to include is the wood element. To ensure it is live wood rather than dead wood, place freshly cut flowers in it. This stimulates a situation when romance is blossoming or is about to blossom.

This little ritual thus creates all five elements of the universe, with the fire element leading the way. The candle represents fire; the semi-precious stones symbolize the earth element; the flowers, wood; the gold, metal; and then there is water. Thus, all five elements are represented, making the symbolism complete and whole.

When the candles have burned out, remove them from the bowl.

This is a very good thing to do when you have friends over for dinner, particularly when someone special is present. It generates the luck of tenderness and encourages the chi of affection to flow gently but strongly, thereby affecting everyone in the room. You might wish to try organizing a small get-together like this during one evening of the full moon to see what the evening brings romantically!

The mystic knot brings endless love

The love knot
Place a picture of this mystic knot in your bedroom to help promote a long, loving relationship with your partner.

The mystic knot is sometimes called the endless knot as it is said to "swallow its own tail". The esoteric meaning of this symbol implies there is no beginning and no end – reflecting the Buddhist philosophy that existence is one endless round of birth and rebirth – a state the Buddhists refer to as samsara.

The knot is therefore a wonderful reminder that once we realize this great noble truth about existence we will start to seek for methods to be free of the endless cycle of births and rebirths.

Buddhists of all traditions seek to attain this freedom. The endless knot symbol is also seen on the breast of the Hindu deity Vishnu, and it is also one of the eight signs on the sole of Buddha's feet.

At a less spiritual level, the mystic knot is often identified with endless love, a love so great it has no beginning and no end, and this is what makes it such a romantic symbol. Place it in your bedroom to symbolize a long relationship with your loved one uninterrupted by separations, setbacks or sufferings.

The lucky knot

Because of its place in spiritual tradition this knot is often regarded as a lucky knot. It is therefore a very popular ornamental symbol that is used in a variety of ways – carved onto furniture, woven into carpets, embroidered onto garments, and painted on screens.

If you like it, you may use it freely in your home and place it especially in the south-west corner of your bedroom. The mystic knot is much like the double happiness symbol. It brings the kind of happiness that is associated with feeling loved and feeling secure. It is therefore a wonderful symbol to have in the home.

47 Bright garden lights attract proposals

If you want romance and marriage luck, you should definitely install a tall bright light in the south-west corner of your garden. This will not only help to keep the flames of love alive between husband and wife; more excitingly, it can enhance the marriage prospects of all the eligible members of the household – all the sons and daughters of marriageable age will not lack for serious suitors with honourable intentions!

In fact, lights in the south-west, placed in any way, anywhere, always represent auspicious luck regarding family and marriage of a home's residents, unless other sectors are afflicted, or when astrological charts show severe mismatches. However, even then, these lights help to reduce differences, thereby creating harmony in relationships.

For these lights to have maximum potency, they should stand at least 1.5–1.8 metres (5–6ft) above the ground and 1m (3ft) below. At the top end of the pipe, have a bright yellow round light – globe-like, if possible – as this is the most auspicious simulating earth energy. The light is thought to represent yang chi. It entices the chi from deep inside the earth to rise up, thereby activating the chi that symbolizes the luck of this sector.

If you are greedy, you can have a cluster of three round lights. Also, remember that roundness is the shape that signifies the purity and power of Heaven Luck. This simple light, in a sense, actually brings about the union of heaven and earth. It is, therefore, very auspicious.

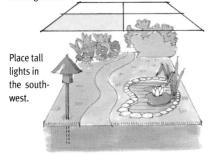

Love light
A tall, bright light positioned in the south-west of the garden will enhance a relationship and bring marriage luck.

Place tall lights in the south-west.

48 Oranges bring good husbands

It is a good idea to lavishly display oranges in the home during Chinese New Year, and to perform a marriage-energizing ritual on the final day – this is the fifteenth day of the New Year. It is also a full moon. In this ritual, juicy oranges are thrown into the nearest large expanse of water.

While throwing the orange into the water, close your eyes and make a wish, visualizing yourself with the kind of person you want as a life partner. Do this at night when the waters are bathed in the silver light of the moon, and let the waters carry the orange into the great unknown. The Chinese believe this ritual brings good husbands to young girls.

Oranges are regarded as being a fruit that signifies gold – which in turn is another word for extreme good fortune. This is because the word for orange is "kum" which is also the word for gold. The orange is very auspicious and is essential for Chinese New Year festivities, ensuring that there will be happiness.

Asking the God of Marriage's help

Yes there *is* a God of Marriage, so all you singles take heart! He is called Chieh Lin, and he is none other than the old man in the moon. He is believed to be in charge of all nuptials between mortals, reputedly sanctioning unions between potential couples on earth by figuratively tying their feet together with an invisible red silk cord.

This belief provides the origin for the bride and groom at Chinese weddings sealing their marriage pledge to each other by drinking wine from two glasses that are tied together with red cord. To activate romance luck in your home, therefore, it is an excellent idea to display a painting of the full moon. Such an image actually signifies yang in yin, and, during the fifteenth day of each Chinese month (when the moon is full), this becomes an auspicious time for undertaking all projects that relate to matters of the heart.

Left: At Chinese weddings, couples emphasize their wedding vows by drinking champagne from two glasses tied together with red cord.

Red for yang energy

I have also heard that placing the old man in the moon in the south-west corner of the house is most auspicious for romance. However, while I have heard many references to this God of Marriage, I have never seen an image of him, so, apart from knowing who and what he is, I am unable to offer a visual description of him, despite much research on the matter.

A more down-to-earth and practical suggestion is to use a lot of vermilion in the south-west to jazz up this corner's fire energy. As any Chinese person knows, red has always been the colour of happiness and joy.

So, to energize romance and marriage luck, introduce curtains, wallpaper and carpets that are vermilion in colour. The vermilion red of fire produces earth in the productive cycle of the elements, and this, together with the strong presence of yang, should successfully activate the south-west area. Do all this in the living room of your home, and not your bedroom. When there is too much yang energy in the bedroom, you will find it difficult to have a good night's sleep.

50 Energizing for love means families

In the language of feng shui, love always implies family – and the luck of contracting a happy marriage that is blessed with many children, especially lots of sons. So, all love energizers bring marriage opportunities to unmarried single men and women. They also enhance love and commitment between spouses.

So if you use feng shui-inspired symbols to animate romance chi this implies that you want a permanent commitment. When you do this the Chinese view is that there is no room for frivolous dalliances. Marriage is regarded as sacred, and infidelity, as we know it, did not exist. Chinese society, in the past, was polygamous, and men frequently had multiple wives and concubines, who were all all considered part of the family. You need to be careful and should not overdo the use of love symbols, as they may result in people developing insatiable appetites that lead to roving eyes. It is also necessary to take simple precautions to ensure that any outside third-party interference is nipped in the bud before it becomes serious enough to break up the marriage or relationship.

Activating for love brings marriage opportunities, but it does not, however, guarantee a permanent commitment that will necessarily last forever. Also, while feng shui can help to attract commitment and serious relationship, it cannot guarantee the quality of the mate – this depends on your own karma.

51 Yang chi to find a husband

Below: For romance, light up your south-west corner and display male and female art.

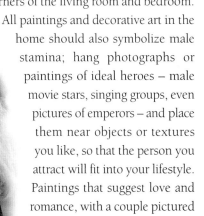

Single women who live alone and are looking for love and marriage should reinforce the masculine yang intensity of the energies in their homes. One way to ensure this is to place a bright lamp in the south-west corners of the living room and bedroom. All paintings and decorative art in the home should also symbolize male stamina; hang photographs or paintings of ideal heroes – male movie stars, singing groups, even pictures of emperors – and place them near objects or textures you like, so that the person you attract will fit into your lifestyle. Paintings that suggest love and romance, with a couple pictured in them, should occasionally be displayed, as they lend balance to energies. Music in the house is good "life energy", and things in pairs balance any decorative display. Avoid excessively yin decorations, such as dark colours, minimalist design, and rice-coloured Japanese shades, since these suggest yin chi. Black furniture or carpets should always be balanced with strong, not harsh lighting, so that the room is well lit.

To be safe, implement these energizing ideas in your living room, not your bedroom. Guard against making your bedroom too yang, as this encourages aggression in the search for a mate, possibly deterring potential suitors. Also, do not paint your bedroom red or display dragons in your bedroom if you are still unmarried.

Bachelor apartments need feminine energy

Above and below: Displaying flowers, such as narcissus and peonies, will help to bring a love affair into a bachelor apartment.

Single men living alone should ensure that their homes never lack yin energies. Those wanting to settle down, who cannot find the right girl, should undertake a feng shui analysis of their bachelor pads. In most cases, their living space will have an excess of yang male energy, with the female chi absent or in short supply. I have seen bachelor apartments that are completely empty of objects which emanate female energy.

Male apartments usually have paintings and decorative objects that reflect male interests. Thus, ships, guns, military heroes, and so forth, will tend to dominate. Things like paperweights, briefcases, ashtrays and cigarette boxes are normally present and strongly suggest masculine taste!

In order to draw feminine energies into a space, it is necessary to simulate the female presence. Symbols associated with feminine efficacy are sculptures, portraits and paintings of women. It is an excellent idea to hang artwork that depicts the female form. However, do not display antique paintings of old women. You should also not hang paintings that portray scenes from Chinese classics like *The Dream of the Red Chamber*, since the women depicted in many of these stories are not women you would want to marry. Many are "foxes" – spirit-women who entice men for their temporary enjoyment. Recall, also, the legend of the white snake, who changed into a beautiful woman to snare a student.

Using art and flowers

When hanging art to gain feng shui benefits, new art is always better than old art, unless you know the exact provenance of old pieces. It is the same with furniture.

A home should hold the symbolic presence of flowers, as they signify beautiful women or romance. The best flowers to display are peonies, since these are powerful emblems of conjugal love. There are also flowers that signify married couples: the narcissus (also an excellent energizer for careers when displayed during the lunar New Year period), the plum blossom, and the orchid. A picture showing the narcissus and peony together signifies an impending marriage, while orchids with peonies symbolize a romance between two people whose families are close friends.

53 Personal love symbols for romance

Symbolism in feng shui affects the quality of energies; the stronger the belief systems surrounding symbols, usually the stronger will be the energies created by them. It is a mistake to think that only Chinese images work. Look for symbols of romance in your own culture and belief systems. For example, you can use red hearts and western lovebirds in place of double-happiness and phoenix symbols when you wish to energize romance luck for your friends or family.

Indeed, some of the most powerful symbols of love that I have encountered are western. I am not referring to sexually charged paintings alone (although those as well), but to true masterpieces which suggest conjugal love or family happiness. One of these is Gustav Klimt's The Kiss – a stunning painting with awesome power to suggest intense and exciting romance, which I have always loved. When you come across any painting that moves you with its romanticism, do buy it and hang it in your home. Remember, different people find different things romantic!

Another powerful energizer of love chi that was invented in the West is the crystal chandelier – itself an excellent feng shui symbol, because it signifies the yang energy of earth having come alive. If you cannot afford something elaborate, look for smaller substitutes. They can be quite affordable.

Below: Hang pictures of loving couples in your home to symbolize love and commitment. Here is my favourite, The Kiss, by Gustav Klimt.

Personal power

Remember that, when you energize for love, you yourself will be the most powerful enhancer of the energies of your space. Many people forget this is one of the things that makes symbolic feng shui work so well. The human psyche energizes strongly through its own belief systems. By understanding the basis of the symbolic meanings that lie behind objects, we empower the objects with positive accumulations of chi energy. This, when applied with proper feng shui understanding of the five elements (or wu xing), in turn, attracts into our world wonderful happiness luck. So, when energizing spaces for romance, do not be afraid to allow room for creativity!

Fine-tune with trigrams

It is possible to use trigram arrangements in the yang Pa Kua to fine-tune your love feng shui. Under the yang Pa Kua, the arrangement of the trigrams are laid out according to what is known as the earthly sequence. In this arrangement, the trigram Kun is placed in the south-west (see sketch). Note also the names of the other trigrams and their placement in the different sectors. This will help you to understand how different hexagrams are made for the eight door directions.

The south-west corner

The normal feng shui practice is to identify the south-west corner of any home or apartment, and then to proceed to activate or energize that corner in order to attract romance luck. However, it is also possible to fine-tune an analysis of the luck of anyone's home, including romance luck, by superimposing the fixed Pa Kua method onto the yang Pa Kua. The fixed Pa Kua method of determining door locations assumes the corners of the Pa Kua to be "fixed" in relation to the main door. This could have been the original basis of the practice, which may have been followed by feng shui practitioners who assumed the front door is always sitting north and facing south. The Yang Pa Kua (shown above here) representing Earth is the Pa Kua used to analyze homes.

By superimposing the fixed Pa Kua over the moving yang Pa Kua, it is possible to

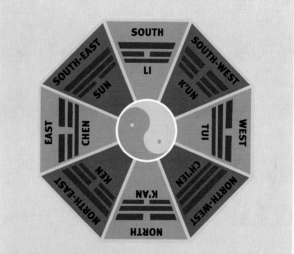

Using the yang Pa Kua

The arrangement of the trigrams in this Pa Kua indicates the various meanings of the compass sectors. They are as follows:

South with the trigram Li which represents recognition and fame

North with the trigram Kan which represents careers and work

East with the trigram Chen which represents health and longevity

West with the trigram Tui which represents children and the next generation

South-west with the trigram Kun which represents relationships, love and marriage

South-east with the trigram Sun which represents wealth and prosperity

North-west with the trigram Chien which represents mentors and helpful, powerful people

North-east with the trigram Ken which represents wisdom, education and study

analyze the kind of love luck that residents can enjoy by checking the direction the main door faces. The door directions of different houses determines how the trigrams of the yang Pa Kua move. From this, a hexagram can be constructed which governs the luck of love and relationships (as well as other types of luck) for different houses, based on their door directions.

55 Double romance luck with the two Pa Kuas

In normal feng shui practice you would use a compass to identify the south-west corner of any home, and then "energize" that corner to attract romance luck – there are lots of ways to do this. However, you can fine-tune your love feng shui by finding a second love corner – after all, two can be more powerful than one!

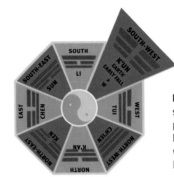

Left: In feng shui, the Pa Kua is usually shown with north in the "south" position. The trigrams on the Pa Kua can be used to find solutions to problems with the love sector of your home, or to boost existing energies.

Using the Pa Kuas

First of all, identify your south-west corner using a compass. Trace off the Pa Kua diagram (right) and overlay it on a simple plan of your house or apartment, matching up the south-west corners (You will need two copies of your house plan). You will see that the south-west sector on the Pa Kua is represented by the trigram Kun, which represents relationships, love and marriage (see Pa Kua, above). Also, note the names of the other trigrams and see where they fall in the other areas of your home – this will give you a basic understanding of the directions chart in Tip 56.

Next, take the second copy of your house or apartment plan. This time, imagine that your front door faces south, so when you walk into your home you are facing north. Mark the south-west corner on your plan – this will be to the left of the front door. Then take the plan and lay it over the first plan – don't align the directions, just overlay them so the layout of the rooms matches up. You will see that you have two love sectors now – one in the "real" south-west, as defined by your compass reading, and one in the south-west to the left of your front door. Place Kun in this new sector and note the trigram now in in the original love sector, this trigram placed above trigam Kun gives the hexagram for your location. Look up in Tip 56 to find

Geographical or yang Pa Kua

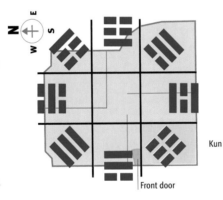

Front door

Kun

Front door

Fixed "Front Door" Pa Kua

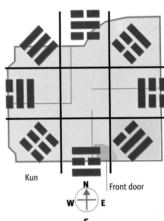

Kun

Kun

Front door

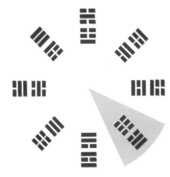

Left: Combine the two Pa Kuas to create the hexagram for your specific location.

Sun

Kun

Left: Remember, when you look at a complete Pa Kua you view the symbols from the centre, so turn the hexagrams so that you place Kun beneath Sun.

out a feng shui tip that will really maximize your love potential!

Now re-interpret your combined houseplan as if the front door faces

south, as on the second plan. This changes the direction of the "real" south-west, so that you end up with a new direction.

How doors affect marriage prospects

The chart below summarizes the effects of the moving yang Pa Kua when it is superimposed onto the fixed Pa Kua. This concerns the effect of door directions on the marriage prospects of residents. If the home is inhabited by no one of marriageable age, the absence of good marriage luck should not be a problem, but when there are several young sons and daughters present, then remedies should be found to overcome this marriage affliction. If their marriage prospects are good, they can be made better by energizing certain corners. Please check the summary of recommendations below.

When door direction faces: Marriage prospects of residents is	Ruling hexagram, I Ching number (#) and meaning	Best remedies
SOUTH Excellent marriage prospects. (south-west in south-west)	Kun on Kun # 2 The matriarch doubled. Must take the initiative.	Make better by energizing the west with wind chimes. To persevere will be of benefit.
NORTH Not so good. Residents too analytical and also too choosy. (north-east in south-west)	Ken on Kun # 23 No support. Unfavourable luck for marriage.	Energize for some wisdom luck. Place a crystal in the north-east and lights in the south-west.
EAST Not so good, but can get help from older friends and parents. (north-west in south-west)	Chien on Kun # 12 Relationships tend to stagnate. Progress only in small doses.	Place a strong six-rod wind chime in the north-west. Should try to strengthen north-west
WEST Neither good nor bad. Better for second marriage. (south-east in south-west)	Sun on Kun # 20 Marriage luck is man-made.	Place a wind chime in the west if you want to get married very badly.
SOUTH-EAST Success luck. Good social life with lots of friends. (east in south-west)	Tui on Kun # 45 Good beneficial luck. Love comes from all directions.	Place fire element in the east sector.
SOUTH-WEST Either very good or very bad. The implication is too much noise. Too much gossip or maybe a lot of fame. (south in south-west)	Li on Kun # 35 Will either be an outstanding match for son or daughter of the house OR scandal.	Place water in the south to keep fire under control.
NORTH-EAST Can find love at work. Marriage luck is neutral. (north in south-west)	Kan on Kun # 8 Good union luck. Wonderful indications for marriage chi.	Place water feature in north. but place lots of love and romance energizers in the south-west.
NORTH-WEST Excellent for those who want to marry into wealth. (west in south-west)	Chen on Kun # 16 Denotes excellent happiness. No problem getting married.	Energize the south-east with plants and bright lights to crystallize luck. Also place lights in the south-west.

57 Magnifying love luck with the two Pa Kuas

When you have assessed your door directions and found your ruling hexagram (see Tips 55 and 56) you can maximize the energy in your home to create even better opportunities for love. You can use "energizers" such as crystals and wind-chimes, bright lights and plants, and also use the elements to boost or calm the energy in a certain sector of the home. For example, you can place water features to calm chi or use symbols of the fire element, such as the colour red, to magnify chi energy.

You can also work on more than one corner of your home. Bear in mind that using the hexagrams in this way really helps to fine-tune love and relationship feng shui and is an advanced technique. If you can't use all the energizers listed for your door direction in the chart in Tip 56, don't worry – remember that using a water feature, for example, can be as

Above: For north-east door directions, place a water feature such as goldfish in the north, and love and romance energizers, such as hanging crystals, in the south-west.

Left: The trigram Kan over the Kun trigram represents good partnership luck.

Right: If your door direction is north-west, placing a bright light in the south-east is excellent for marrying someone wealthy.

Right: The trigrams Chen on Kun indicate great love and happiness.

simple as placing a small bowl of water in the relevant corner, rather than installing an elaborate fountain! Equally, using bright lights can be as simple as changing the shade on a table lamp from dark blue to pale yellow or orange.

Although these changes may appear minor, they will have the effect of making the most of all the positive love and marriage energies around you.

Change your door and find a soul mate

One method of enhancing your relationship or marriage chances is to do something about your door directions, i.e., the door going into your home as well as the door into your bedroom. You have seen from the previous page that doors which face north and east, for instance, are not so good for creating good luck regarding love – although they may well create extreme good fortune in other areas of your life. Discovering this requires further and deeper analysis that is not within the scope of this particular book.

However, if love is what you want, and finding a partner or soul mate is at the top of your list of priorities, then you may wish to seriously consider one of the following options:

If you live alone in an apartment and need not worry about the effect on other residents' feng shui, you can change your front door direction. But only take this option if you can actually change to a better direction that is also good for you according to your year of birth (see Chapter Four to find your best love direction). Also, there are only two possibilities to consider for a change in door direction. You either shift the door's orientation to open to the left or the right. It is not possible to change the direction of doors too dramatically, unless you have a house and there is an alternative door that you can convert to become your main door.

If you live with others, you can consider changing the direction of your bedroom door. There is a novel way of creating a "second" entrance into your room with floor-to-ceiling curtains. Once again, you should check your personal best direction to make sure that any change does not harm you, based on the Eight Mansions KUA formula (given in Chapter Four).

You may also change apartments altogether if other things are wrong with where you live and you are renting the place. Sometimes this is the best and easiest solution, especially for single people.

If you live with your parents, consider moving to another bedroom with a door direction that has better romance luck.

Tip 56 gives you a couple of options to consider regarding changing door directions.

Changing door directions

You can change a bad door direction to your home if you can adjust it to a more auspicious one for you. This can be done simply by adding a screen behind the door which changes the flow of chi as it comes in (see above right). Alternatively, you can build a porch (see right) to achieve the direction that you want.

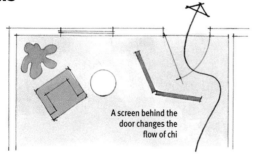

A screen behind the door changes the flow of chi

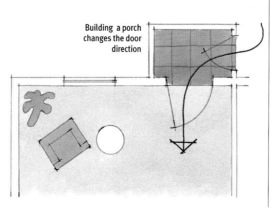

Building a porch changes the door direction

59

Finding love at work

Above: The trigrams Tui on kun.

Below: To find a love partner through your job, try to work in a room that faces north-west and stimulate the east with some red objects.

If you enjoy your work and like the people you interact with, you may find love in the office. When you like your colleagues and get on well with them, it might not be a bad idea to regard your work-place as somewhere for finding meaningful romance.

A good way to encourage an office friendship and help it blossom into love and commitment is to use the feng shui techniques in this section of the book, which focus on showing you how you can fine-tune your love luck. First of all, continue to energize the south-west sector of your home in accordance with the tips given in Chapter Two, but also take note of the recommendations and the special energizing methods given here in order to get what you want.

Love in the office

In order to create the chi of romance at work, start by using a door that faces south-east. This is a very powerful door for attracting friends and marriage opportunities from all directions, but, in addition, it activates relationship luck at work, thereby enhancing the possibility of a friendship at the office blossoming into love and commitment.

So, if there is someone at work you are especially fond of, or you are attracted to, try to see if you can find a room with a door facing north-west. This can be your bedroom door at home, or it can be the door into your office. If you cannot find such a door, then sit facing north-west to activate this luck. Obviously, the best situation would be if the door into your home was facing north-west – in which case, you should activate the east sector of your home or office with an object that suggests the fire element. This could be anything that is red in colour – perhaps a lamp, a painting or curtains. (To determine these directions, see Tips 55 and 56, which summarize the fixed and moving Pa Kua methods of analysis for types of luck.)

In the meantime, don't forget to also make sure that you are creating good personal love luck for yourself by following your KUA direction on love (see the instructions in Tip 68).

Marry into money by moving doors

If you want to marry into money, then you should actively look for or create a door direction that is conducive to such an event happening. Wealth coming from marriage and love is activated when your main door faces the north-west.

This creates the hexagram Yu, shown here, which means happiness. Yu is made up of the trigram Chen sitting upon the trigram Kun. It symbolizes thunder rising from earth – and a loud noise is heard for many miles around. Representing a time of new beginnings, it symbolizes enthusiasm, exuberance and a state of supreme happiness. It also suggests great success and wealth. However, the hidden meaning of this hexagram also warns against over-indulgence which can lead to poor health, limitations and also misfortunes. The hexagram is a particularly wise one because it symbolizes and predicts initial intense happiness, while also warning against the delusion that wealth can last forever. It implies that having a correct attitude is the best way for good fortune to continue.

Marrying into wealth

A main door facing north-west is said to attract "big gold" into the household through the home's offspring contracting what in the past would have been described as "a fantastic match". It means that a family's children marry extremely well. If the west is also a favourable direction for them, the good fortune is further magnified and compounded.

Those of you with serious aspirations for your son or daughter to find a good match might also want to make sure that the south-

Above: Hanging a clear, crystal chandelier in the south-west of your home can energize the area and help your marriage prospects.

Below: The trigrams Chen on Kun.

west corner of your home is being properly energized with a beautiful, well-growing plant. You can also place a gem tree in the south-west to complement the real plant in the south-east. At the same time, hang a bright crystal chandelier in the south-west.

Please remember, however, that marrying into wealth does not guarantee either an eternally happy marriage or an especially romantic match. Wealth on its own does not create happiness. If you also wish for the match to be fruitful and happy, it is important to ensure that the rest of your home also enjoys good feng shui, and that, more importantly, the whole of the marital home is properly planned according to feng shui principles.

61 Find true love with inner feng shui

Not everyone wants a socially successful marriage that makes good press, satisfies older generations, yet brings little of the kind of happiness associated with love and romance. If all you want is to find true love – then, rather than create feng shui for marriage, you should create feng shui for happiness. This will engage your inner spiritual side, which will know what happiness means to you.

Finding happiness with someone you love is not just about spatial feng shui. You have to also use inner feng shui – the feng shui of your mind – which involves creating vivid mental "pictures" of your ideal man or woman. This must be partly your own effort and, therefore, requires you to feng shui your mind as well as your space.

Regarding the spatial aspects of your home, I strongly recommend that you observe all the feng shui tips already given. Then create the opportunity to live in a home with the main door facing south. But first, check that south is a favourable direction for you, based on your

Above: To activate love, boost the matriarchal energy – try to live in a home with a south facing door and enhance the west with wind chimes.

Above: The doubled trigram Kun.

KUA formula (see Tip 68); if it is, great! Look for a south-facing door. This will create the wonderful hexagram, Kun, for your love luck, which is a doubled Kun trigram. This hexagram is a very auspicious one and it suggests benefits gained from tenacity. Indeed, to find true love, you must persevere and not give up. The man or woman of your dreams does exist. You simply have to work harder to find him or her! You must be like the earth that provides sustenance for everything. The poetry of this hexagram is really very beautiful, because it describes the universal attributes of loving kindness – the type that is usually associated with the matriarch, the receptive, that which can bear anything.

Boosting your love luck

After this, enhance your love luck further by energizing the western sector with wind chimes. This not only introduces balance to the power created by earth doubled, it also symbolizes finding gold – achieving what you set out to do.

If you can, also have your bedroom door facing south, as this strengthens the essence of the Kun hexagram in your life. After doing these things, take a deep breath and relax. Do not impart negative energies to your feng shui by constantly wondering when things will happen. The common mistake which many people make when they use feng shui is that they keep anticipating meeting someone. Stop thinking about it, stay relaxed and don't be so busy anticipating that you miss noticing the man or woman of your dreams! I have known this to happen.

Energizing for a successful mate

If you are someone who likes living in reflected glory, and want nothing more than to be a good partner to a successful person, one way of encouraging this is to live in a house with a door that faces south-west. The hexagram for this kind of love luck is described as: "being bestowed with many horses by the king". This description suggests being given something that is, perhaps, a little awe-inspiring, which is exactly the feeling often engendered when you get together with someone who is a great achiever.

The hexagram, Li on Kun (see Tip 63), is visually depicted as fire rising above the earth, and this suggests the advent of fame (or notoriety) brought about by marriage. As a hexagram of love, it is neither very good nor very bad; it is, in fact, both. Depending on other factors, people of marriageable age who live in a home with the main door facing south-west can either make a totally brilliant match, marrying far above themselves both socially and financially, or they could well suffer a scandal associated with sex and infidelity. The implication here is that there could be too much noise, excessive gossip and, perhaps, too many disturbances from outsiders, resulting in jealousy and betrayal.

Using water to calm yang

It would be a good idea to place some still water in the south, thereby keeping the fire that rises above the earth a little under control. This will reduce the excessive yang of this hexagram, and lead to better fortunes that are also more balanced. Make sure that the water is not bubbling, oxygenated water, as this disturbs the energy of the south. An aquarium, therefore, would not be suitable for this purpose. An urn or jug filled with water would be ideal.

Use this suggestion if you are presently in a situation that reflects the description given here. If your wife or husband is more successful than you are, you can use feng shui to even matters out a little. In fact, this will bring about a far happier marriage.

Those who have successful husbands can create a great deal of family luck for themselves so that, along with the luck of the patriarch, luck will also come for the family. Lighting the south-west corner with bright lights should also energize the luck of the matriarch.

Those with successful wives must immediately activate the north-west corner of their homes. Hang a large wind chime in this corner to create yang energy. Ensure that all major door directions are auspicious for you and your husband, and energize your success luck.

Below: Energizing your south-west corner of your living room with candles can help to enhance matriarch luck.

63 Marrying into fame

A south-west-facing door is said to bring the sun to that part of the house. When a residence's main door faces south-west, it is likely that one of its inhabitants will marry someone that is famous.

The ruling hexagram of love and marriage luck created by a south-west door direction is shown here. This is the hexagram Chin, which means progress. It is symbolized by the sun shining brightly above the earth, which denotes a brightness (i.e., positive yang energy) that is associated with mother earth.

An obvious interpretation of this symbolism is fame through marriage. It does not mean that everyone with such a door will marry into fame, but the odds are high that they will. So if your astrological chart supports such a thing happening, a door with this orientation will surely make the karma ripen.

Some *I Ching* masters, however, interpret a south-west-facing door as one which brings fame to the women of a household. This is

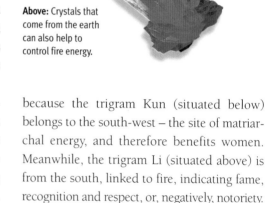

Above: Crystals that come from the earth can also help to control fire energy.

because the trigram Kun (situated below) belongs to the south-west – the site of matriarchal energy, and therefore benefits women. Meanwhile, the trigram Li (situated above) is from the south, linked to fire, indicating fame, recognition and respect, or, negatively, notoriety.

Female success

Since, in the past, women neither had careers nor management jobs, success for women usually meant marrying a husband who was destined for high office or marrying into a prominent family. Today this kind of feng shui interpretation has a wider range of meaning. In the context of modern times, women need not gain fame or success only through marriage.

In addition, in the modern world, marrying into fame does have its hazards and, if this happens to you, it is a good idea to ensure that the excessive heat of too much fire does not harm your home. Place water in the south to curb fame's fire energy. Or you could exhaust the fire by setting earth or a small mound of rocks there, so that you do not put out the fire with water, but merely control it.

Above: Li above Kun produces the hexagram Chin for progress.

Right: Putting some stones in the south will help to keep fame's fire under control.

North-facing doors are not good for romance

When your main door faces north, there is a danger that the house's residents will have a hard time finding partnerships that satisfy them. In this situation, the hexagram on love is the inauspicious one called Po, which, literally, means "disintegrating". It does not spell good luck in your relationships, and generally indicates situations of extreme negativity. This hexagram (shown below right) has the mountain sitting above the earth, i.e., the trigram Ken above Kun. Here, a lone mountain indicates loneliness and lack of support or friends.

This is not a good situation, and you must take steps to either find another room with a door direction that is more conducive to love, or immediately place a crystal in the north-east corner of your room or home. Also light up the south-west corner with bright lights.

Unlucky relationships

If you are a bachelor, the indication of this hexagram is that you have many frivolous and extremely shallow relationships, but none of your friends will like you enough to marry you. In fact, if your other luck is also bad, you could get cheated by women. They will betray you and take you for a ride. If you are a woman, the likelihood is that you will have more women friends than men friends.

The best recommendation I can give in this situation is to make your main door face either north-east or north-west, i.e., tilt the direction of the entrance door a little bit (about 45 degrees), either to the left or right, to improve your relationship luck. But do remember that changing door directions is a serious step and requires an investigation into your auspicious directions also. If the north-west or north-east is also auspicious for you, then it is a good idea to go ahead.

In the meantime, do energize the south-west corner with mandarin ducks, and create lots of yang energy in the home with lights, sounds and more life. This means, if you live alone, you may want to find yourself a pet, such as a cat or dog.

Above: If you live in your home on your own, a pet can bring in positive, bustling yang energy as well as giving love and affection.

Below: Ken on Kun makes the inauspicious hexagram Po.

65 Windchimes overcome stagnating love chi

Those of you who live in homes with an east-facing front door generally suffer from "afflicted" relationship luck. The tendency is for most of your relationships to lack the vibrancy and energy necessary for them to move forward. So this means there is a tendency towards stagnation. The ruling hexagram on relationships is, in fact, Pi, which literally means "stagnation".

Left: By putting a six-rod wind chime in the north-west area of your home you can force stagnant chi to move freely again.

The Pi hexagram

This is represented here and you will see that the trigram Chien sits above Kun. It represents the classical situation where strength on the outside hides weakness on the inside, and denotes situations that have no inherent foundation, which can easily collapse. In relationships, this spells disaster.

Having disposed of the bad news, we can now move on to the good news. Those with this affliction can overcome the stagnating chi by forcing it to move. Activate the Chien trigram by strengthening the north-west. Place a strong six-rod wind chime in the north-west of your home, as well as in the north-west of your bedroom. Make the six rods hollow to call forth the energy of the sector. Six is the number of this sector, and hollow rods force the chi to move. Also, try to make the wind chimes tinkle. Use a fan to blow the chimes.

Older mentors

By energizing in this way, you will attract the help of older friends. Be open to introductions, blind dates and chance meetings. Be open also to suggestions from parents, aunts and uncles. When offers from them are made, do not shrug them off, since this is only the north-west chi helping you along. If you like, you can also place music in the north-west to activate the corner even more. Do not use lights here, since the fire element of light will destroy the metal element of this corner. For the same reason, also, do not place water in this area, as water will exhaust metal. Instead, help the metal element with crystals – good earth energy.

Door location implications for love

Based on the location of the doors in your home, it is possible to read the kind of relationship luck and attitudes that tend to pervade a household. Please note that a differentiation is made between location and compass direction. The summary here is based on further readings of the derivations of the ruling hexagrams, which govern love luck. This method of feng shui is based directly on the *I Ching's* hexagrams and is different from other formulas and techniques. Readers need not be confused by the different feng shui methods; this is a 4,000-year-old science and, to a large extent, most of its techniques are related and linked through the use of similar symbols and tools. Their main differences arise from interpretations and practical applications. These differ according to the lineage from which they have been derived.

The table on the right summarizes the effects of door locations on general attitudes towards love and relationships.

If door is located in the: ... the general tendency is ...

SOUTH:
To take the romantic view. A rather aggressive approach to love which bears fruit. Love luck is good, but must guard against being obsessed by love and romance. Should stay cool.

NORTH:
To be very sensible about love – maybe too sensible. Dangerous when this is taken to extremes; being picky and choosy will cause you to lose out in the love stakes. Remember, relationships work both ways.

EAST:
To prevaricate and wait for others to take the initiative. Result is that relationships usually wither and die. Could get help from older relatives and friends, but must take the initiative and strengthen yang energy. Listlessness and laziness will not get you married!

WEST:
Attitude to love fluctuates with the mood of the moment. This is neither good nor bad, but you have to create your own luck. Here, also, children could be the catalyst.

SOUTH-EAST:
A very flirtatious and vivacious approach to love and romance. Looks for love in all places. Very open-minded – sometimes too much so. Should be more choosy and discerning.

NORTH-EAST:
A sociable approach is taken. Usually popular with work-mates and colleagues, and can well find romance at the office or through work-related meetings.

SOUTH-WEST:
Aims high. Rather ambitious and snooty. But luck is on his/her side. Usually, also, the head rules the heart, and enjoys the support of marriage luck!

NORTH-WEST:
Usually tends to be a social-climber but, again, love luck tends to be good. Could marry above their social status. But should be careful about health. Love could lead to difficult health-oriented problems.

Left: Where your front door is positioned can have a bearing on how your relationships progress.

67 Love energizers for the main door

In the practice of feng shui, there are two approaches to take when energizing for any kind of luck. One approach is to install remedies that dissolve and reduce afflicted chi. The other is to physically rearrange and/or change your surroundings.

Bad chi that results in varying degrees of bad luck is caused by a door direction being inauspicious or to a good door being harmed by external hostile structures. Sometimes it is due to element imbalance, and other times to an imbalance of yin or yang.

Here, we are addressing deficiencies and abundance in love luck – caused by door directions alone. The idea is to make up for bad luck and to magnify good luck.

Below: If your main door is facing north or south-east, energize the south-west and south-east with some lights or candles.

If the main door is located or facing: Things to energize for a safe, happy love life ...

SOUTH:
Create balance by activating the chi in the north-east with crystals. This brings about a more sensible attitude towards love. You will not be so obsessed with romance, or so forward.

NORTH:
Learn to let go a little bit and don't be so uptight. Activate the south-west strongly with symbols, for example lovebirds and hearts. Install bright lights.

EAST:
Energize the north-west with a metal wind chime. The idea is to strengthen the north-west sector as much as possible. No lights or water here!

WEST:
You will benefit by placing strong metal objects in the west sector. A large wind chime is a good idea, but a stereo system or some bells here will also benefit your love life.

SOUTH-EAST:
You may want to consider placing some lights in the south-east to ripen the luck of this corner. At the same time, some quiet water (i.e., non-bubbling) is also helpful here.

NORTH-EAST:
Place a water feature in the north to activate the chi in this sector. This strengthens the environment within which love is to be found, but also reinforce the south-west with crystals. This way, the energies here stay balanced.

SOUTH-WEST:
A little bit of water in the south to quell fire stops it from becoming too strong. But also place crystals in the south-west to continue fanning relationship luck.

NORTH-WEST:
Activate the chi of the east with healthy growing plants: young plants for younger people and older plants for older people.

How to calculate your personal KUA number

In the Eight Mansions, or Pa Kua Lo Shu, method of feng shui, the personal marriage corner of individuals can be determined according to their date of birth and gender. You can use this very powerful method of feng shui to play Cupid in your life. To do this, you will need to determine the lunar year of your birth. This generally corresponds to the western calendar, except that you must adjust for the Chinese New Year date of your particular year of birth. Check your lunar year of birth very carefully by referring to the lunar New Year dates of each year given in the calendar at the front of this book, and then use the formula here to determine your KUA number. Remember that, if you were born before the New Year, you need to deduct one year from your year of birth before applying the formula here.

Above: To boost your chances of marriage or an enduring relationship, work out your KUA number so that you can determine your personal love corner.

Check your personal marriage corner from this table:

FOR FEMALES: TAKE THE YEAR OF YOUR BIRTH: Add the last two digits. Keep adding until you get a single digit number. Add 5 and the answer is your KUA number. Example: year of birth 1945. Thus: $4 + 5 = 9$; $9 + 5 = 14$: $1 + 4 = 5$. So the KUA is 5. Note that, for those born in the years 2000 and beyond, instead of adding 5, you add 6.

FOR MALES, TAKE THE YEAR OF YOUR BIRTH: Add the last two digits. Keep adding until you get a single digit number. Deduct from 10. The answer is your KUA number. Example: year of birth 1936. Thus: $3 + 6 = 9$; $10 - 9 = 1$. So the KUA is 1. Please note that for those born in the years 2000 and beyond, instead of deducting from 10, you deduct from 9.

Once you know your personal marriage nien yen (relationship and love) corner, try to make sure that neither the toilet, nor the kitchen, nor the storeroom, is situated in that corner. These press down on or diminish your marriage luck. Also, make sure you do not place things like brooms and mops in this corner. Instead, you should think about activating this corner, and the following pages tell you how!

YOUR KUA NUMBER	YOUR RELATIONSHIP & LOVE CORNER
1	SOUTH
2	NORTH-WEST
3	SOUTH-EAST
4	EAST
5	(MALES) NORTH-WEST
5	(FEMALES) WEST
6	SOUTH-WEST
7	NORTH-EAST
8	WEST
9	NORTH

69

How to activate your personal love corner

Based on the KUA, or Eight Mansions formula, every person has his own relationship and love corner. This lucky direction (location) is referred to as the personal nien yen direction.

There are many different ways of applying nien yen. And all of these applications are associated with creating happiness luck in areas to do with feelings, sentiments and the heart. For those not yet married, nien yen intensifies the luck of romance when it is activated. It also magnifies the luck of family. So, for instance, if you sleep with your head pointed towards your nien yen direction, you will become more family-oriented in your attitudes. You will view your home as a haven, and your parents will tend to communicate well with you. The perspective from the married viewpoint is that marriage luck is more harmonious.

To activate your personal love corner:

1. Calculate your KUA number (see Tip 68).
2. Check your nien yen from the table on the previous page.
3. Get a good compass and determine which corner of your house corresponds to your nien yen direction.
4. Use a Lo Shu grid to superimpose on your house plans. This will be your nien yen location, or personal love corner.
5. Next, activate the corner – based on the corresponding trigrams, lucky numbers and elements of the direction which needs to be activated. These corresponding attributes offer significant clues on how best you can energize the love corner effectively, and they are summarized in the table below for easy reference.

LOVE DIRECTION ...	LUCKY NUMBER	CORRESPONDING ELEMENT	COLOUR	TRIGRAM
SOUTH	NINE (9)	FIRE	RED, ORANGE	LI
NORTH	ONE (1)	WATER	BLACK, BLUE	KAN
EAST	THREE (3)	WOOD	GREEN	CHEN
WEST	SEVEN (7)	METAL	WHITE	TUI
SOUTH-EAST	FOUR (4)	WOOD	GREEN	SUN
SOUTH-WEST	TWO (2)	EARTH	BEIGE, YELLOW	KUN
NORTH-WEST	SIX (6)	METAL	WHITE	CHIEN
NORTH-EAST	EIGHT (8)	EARTH	BEIGE, YELLOW	KEN

70

Energizing corners with colours

Once you have identified exactly which corner needs to be activated, try to incorporate aesthetics into your feng shui. Simply using colours and colour combinations to enhance the love corner often does wonders in bringing its energies to life. Use the guidelines provided in the table above and the list (right).

The theory of good and bad colour mixed is based on the elements, and it is best to use combinations of colour to create balance. When thinking of activating your love corner, please note the colours that do not mix auspiciously, and those which do. These are summarized here.

If your love corner is in the:

● South: combine red with green and/or yellow. Avoid blacks and blues.

● North: use black and white, black with metallic colours and blues; avoid yellow and green.

● West and north-west: combine white with yellow and metallic colours, avoiding reds and blacks.

● East and south-east: use green with blue and/or black; do not use green with reds and whites.

● South-west and north-east: Choose combinations of yellow and beige and red; do not use yellow with green or brown.

Activating your love corner with symbols

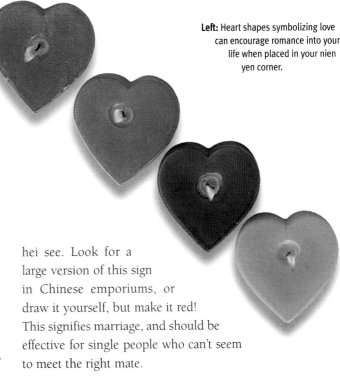

Left: Heart shapes symbolizing love can encourage romance into your life when placed in your nien yen corner.

Your personal marriage corner affects everything regarding your love life and family happiness. When this corner is properly activated, it ensures harmonious family relationships. This direction/location also brings partnership and marriage opportunities to those who are single and of marriageable age, and children to those who may be childless.

Nien yen also improves relationships between couples, and between members of a household. Loosely translated, nien yen actually means "longevity with rich descendants".

Once you know your nien yen direction and corner, you should find the area of your room or home which represents it, and activate it by placing symbols there. Symbols which may be used include those below.

Mandarin ducks are the Chinese symbol of conjugal bliss and often represent young love. Place a pair of carved wooden ducks if the nien yen is in the south, north, east or west direction. They should be made of crystals or semi-precious stones if the nien yen is in the south-west or north-east. For family luck, display a whole family of ducks there. You can set them on a table or on a floor, "swimming" on a square sheet of mirror to simulate water.

Lovebirds or budgerigars may be substituted for mandarin ducks. You can use a picture of a pair of budgies, or carved versions of these beautiful birds. It is not advisable to keep the real thing in cages, as keeping birds in cages does not bring good luck because it represents a lack of freedom.

The double-happiness sign is a symbol for happy occasions – what the Chinese refer to as hei see. Look for a large version of this sign in Chinese emporiums, or draw it yourself, but make it red! This signifies marriage, and should be effective for single people who can't seem to meet the right mate.

Love symbols

Valentine cards or other symbols of love and romance are also excellent energy activators, and it is perfectly acceptable to use your imagination to create new symbols relevant to yourself. You can use wallpaper with heart designs and display a heart-shaped picture frame or music box, or a Chinese love knot.

Roses and peonies signify the universal expression of love and are great for the nien yen corner. It is not necessary to use real roses. Beautiful silk ones will do just as well, and, indeed, are to be preferred, as they never fade! If you put real roses in this corner, do throw them as soon as they fade. Faded flowers are a source of shar chi, which is inauspicious. Also remember to throw away the thorns!

72

Using elements to create love chi

In addition to using traditional symbols of love, there is another dimension to activating romance luck. This involves combining elements with numbers that correspond to your personal nien yen (or love) sector. The table in Tip 68 may be used as a guide for this. In any space that you wish to activate, place objects that reflect the particular element related to the number indicated for that area. In case you are wondering whether to use the whole house as the basis for determining your nien yen, the answer is yes.

However, if the love sector is missing, or is occupied by a toilet, kitchen or garage, you may wish to locate the portion of the living room or bedroom which corresponds to it. I prefer to use the living room whenever I wish to energize

a specific kind of luck, simply because I like to keep my bedroom free of too many different types of chi. Also, there are certain decorative and display objects which are taboo in the bedroom.

When you activate the elements of sectors, it is vital to also take note of other schools of feng shui, since the creation of chi, which is connected with the five elements, is extremely powerful and cuts across all schools of feng shui. For instance, you could inadvertently energize bad luck and strengthen killing chi without knowing it, so you need to be careful.

Below: You can also energize your personal love section with the element relevant to it. But make sure you get it right as you could inadvertently create an unsatisfactory relationship.

Your bedroom and your nien yen

If you have a choice of bedrooms and you wish to activate your marriage luck, then you should choose the room that is situated in the location that corresponds to your nien yen. To determine which room this is, stand in the centre of the house and take directions from there. Use any good western compass for this purpose. Once you discover where the north corner of your home is, you will be able to determine all of its other eight corners. (This exercise is very similar to superimposing the Lo Shu square onto a home to find its various sectors.)

If it is possible to sleep in your nien yen sector and also to sleep with your head pointed in the nien yen direction, then your love and family luck will be magnificently enhanced. Marriage definitely will happen.

This Eight Mansions formula is extremely powerful. It is a simple tool of feng shui and easy to understand. But, in implementing this formula, it is important to locate the correct directions, and equally vital to ensure that nothing is harming your feng shui.

Also, to fine-tune your direction luck, you can take into account the influence of the Three Killings and Five Yellows, both features of Flying Star, an advanced type of feng shui (see Tips 144 and 145).

Auspicious directions

Calculate your KUA number (see Tip 68) and look up your romance directions below. Work out the compass direction of your home to find out if your current bedroom location corresponds, and then check the direction in which you actually sleep.

Your KUA number	Your nien yen or romance direction
1	South
2	North-west
3	South-east
4	East
5	North-west, West
6	South-west
7	North-east
8	West
9	North

Right: Where you have a choice of bedrooms, choose the room that matches your nien yen direction (see left).

74

Energizing for love when out on a date

You can use your personal nien yen to give you some feng shui assistance when you go out on a date. Using your nien yen direction as a guide, refer to the table below for all of the things you can do to help you to activate love and relationship luck.

Wearing good colours

Colours can help the flow of chi within the environment. By wearing the colours that correspond to your personal love directions, you will be enhancing the elements that represent love for your energy field. Some feng shui masters fine-tune this recommendation by adjusting for seasonal changes and varying element strengths within the environment. So, in the summer, for example, the element of fire is strong and it may be advisable not to wear too much red. In the winter, on the other hand, when there is an abundance of water, it is better to wear fire colours, since there is an absence

Above: You can help dates to go well by facing your nien yen direction when eating out, sitting at a table with one of your lucky numbers and by wearing your lucky colours.

of heat. These are the two seasons of the year when big swings in temperature cause great energy imbalances that must be counteracted somehow. The inbetween seasons – Autumn (Fall) and Spring – do not exert such strong seasonal influences on the elements.

Facing personal Directions

This is probably one of the most vital of feng shui recommendations to implement if you are serious about activating romance luck. Always sit facing your nien yen direction, (see Tip 68) or the alternative directions given in the table below. To do this elegantly can sometimes be tricky.

Carry a small compass with you all the time, and make it a habit to always check your directions. I know this sounds silly, but there was a time in my life when I carried a compass and checked my directions constantly. I did this to activate my career luck. Most of the time, I did it so discreetly that people hardly noticed, so I know it is not too hard to do once you get over your initial reluctance to appear strange. Treat it as a joke, but, believe me, using correct directions do bring you a great deal of extreme good fortune.

Colours for dates

If your nien yen direction is:	You should wear this colour on your date:	These are your good numbers:	You should sit facing:
NORTH	Black, Blues or White	1, 6 and 7	NORTH or SOUTH
SOUTH	Reds, Greens	9, 2 and 5	SOUTH or NORTH
EAST and SOUTH-EAST	Greens, Blacks and Blues	3, 4 and 1	EAST or SOUTH-EAST
WEST and NORTH-WEST	Whites, Yellows and lots of glitter	6, 7, 2 and 5	WEST or NORTH-WEST
SOUTH-WEST and NORTH-EAST	Yellows, Orange and Reds	2, 5 and 9	SOUTH-WEST or NORTH-EAST

For passion use fire element in the bedroom 75

The fire element is one of the most powerful elements for bringing about robust romance luck. When placed correctly, and focused in the appropriate direction, lights create yang energy which energizes the love life of everyone within its sphere. But the fire element must be handled with care in the bedroom.

To start with, bright lights are never a good idea in bedrooms. These exude excessive yang and simply lead to sleepless nights, because the mind (and body) is over-stimulated. They do little to attract the kind of romance luck that leads to commitment and a family. When lights are excessively bright, the fire element merely magnifies the male libido.

The fire element should, therefore, be used in conjunction with other important love symbols. The most powerful of these is the double-happiness sign. When this is drawn onto lampshades and lanterns, it creates wonderful and auspicious relationship chi. So, this is the best way to introduce the power of the fire element into the bedroom.

A second method for energizing a bedroom's fire element is to hang red curtains. They should never be over-done, but it is a good idea to hang drapes bearing patterns and symbols of love. Curtains with mandarin ducks, geese and other lovebirds create an ambience for pairs and togetherness, and help to direct yang energy into the kind of luck wanted.

But remember not to introduce the fire element without tempering it with other symbolic love objects.

Left: Bedroom lights can boost your love life, but should be subtle.

Avoid water symbols in the bedroom 76

While the bedroom is an important area to boost marriage luck, you need to be careful when energizing this part of your home. Apart from the symbols mentioned, it can prove harmful to experiment in the bedroom. This is because bad luck in the bedroom can bring about serious illness or cause severe problems between its occupants, which can lead to separation – the separation can even become permanent.

One of the more serious elements that should never be used in the bedroom is water. On a practical level, this means there should be no attempt to place otherwise excellent features of aquariums, ponds, and so forth, there. Unlikely as this may sound, I have actually seen a bedroom with a bed right next to a huge landscaped waterfall. The occupant insisted the sound of water made her sleep well. She also found it terribly romantic – until she discovered that her "loving and romantic" husband had been regularly entertaining other women in their bed.

Pictures of waterfalls, rivers and lakes should also be banned from the bedroom. Another friend of mine, who unwittingly installed an aquarium behind her bed, was robbed three times in two weeks, shortly after installing the aquarium. The spate of bad luck stopped as soon as she threw out the aquarium.

Water in the bedroom does not bring wealth. Instead, it brings loss, illness and infidelities. A glass of water is fine, but avoid water motifs or paintings.

77 Compatibility and the Eight Mansions formula

Above: To have a successful relationship or marriage it is a good idea to find out early on if your partner is the same group as you.

One of the best ways of investigating compatibility is to see whether two people belong to the same group using the Eight Mansions formula, a method which can be used to supplement the animal astrology compatibility readings covered in the next chapter. This method of feng shui divides people into two groups: east and west. Which one you belong to depends on your KUA number. This is calculated according to a formula that uses the individual's year of birth and gender (see Tip 68). With a KUA number, you can tell if you are in the west or east group. Use the table (right) to determine this.

As a general rule, it is always recommended by feng shui masters that people should marry someone from within the same group, because when an east group person marries a west group person, their compatibility will always be put to the test. The feng shui of each clashes seriously with that of the other, so that what is good for one is bad for the other. Door directions, room locations, and sleeping orientations will be good for one while creating problems for the other. Also, there can be no harmony of feng shui cures that will benefit both parties.

Living with incompatabilities

However, once you know that you and your loved one belong to different groups, it is possible to do something about the problem. In such a situation, I recommend that you sleep on two separate beds rather than the same one. This will allow both of you to tap into your own good direction. Also if both of you agree, even have two separate bedrooms. This may seem extreme, but it will, in the long-term, create better relationship luck for you both.

East/west group compatability

If your KUA numbers are:	Your group is:	And your four auspicious directions are:
1, 3, 4 or 9 for men & women	East	South, North, East & South-east
2, 6, 7 or 8 for men & women	West	North-west, South-west, North-east & West
5 for women	West	North-west, South-west, North-east & West
5 for men	West	North-west, South-west, North-east & West

Customizing your feng shui to your horoscope

Working out your feng shui in line with your horoscope requires an understanding of the Chinese lunar calendar. The calendar comprises 60-year cycles, which are made up of ten heavenly stems and twelve earthly branches.

In the 60-year cycle, heavenly stems with either a yin or a yang aspect combine with the twelve branches or animal signs. This interaction of stems and branches represents the interplay of heaven and earthly energies, which in turn determines everyone's destiny. That is why all Chinese divination methods rely, ultimately, on interpreting a person's "stems" and "branches".

These stems and branches can be used to personalize the feng shui of any individual. One popular way to improve your own personal feng shui luck is to energize the compass direction of your home which relates to the animal sign of your year of birth. Each of these animals, starting with the Rat and ending with the Boar, has a corresponding compass direction. This direction indicates his "lucky spot" in the home, and the corner or sector where the energy is especially conducive to bringing good fortune to you.

ANIMAL SIGNS
The corresponding direction is:

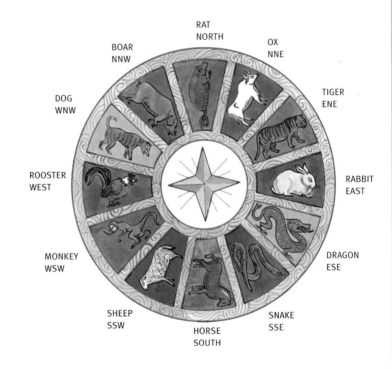

In addition, interaction between different animal signs is also analyzed, with suggestions offered on how best to neutralize the effect of astrological incompatibilities. The directions of animal signs indicate areas in the home which correspond to them, and offer vital clues on where "danger" sectors are within a home during a particular year. So, while it is lucky to place auspicious images in sectors that correspond to your animal sign, it is also vital to check whether any particular direction of yours is afflicted in any given year, and then to identify the animal sign which is affected. This requires observing the three golden rules in Tip 79.

79

Three golden rules for avoiding "Flying Star" danger

When you know the sectors of your home that correspond to your animal sign, you will be able to check to see how you, and the sector that will bring you the most luck, are being affected by what feng shui masters call the "annual danger sectors" in the home. These danger zones change from year to year, and, unless you take note of where they are within your home, you may be affected by them inadvertently and thereby suffer the consequences of bad feng shui.

These areas contain "time dimension stars" that are said to bring problems. Some people call them the Flying Star feng shui taboos of each year. They are very important, and must be noted; this branch of feng shui is part of a very advanced Flying Star practice. I have shown, in the table below, where the three main danger areas are for each year. These are sectors that are occupied by the Grand Duke Jupiter, the Three Killings and the Deadly Five Yellow. Irrespective of what your KUA number and lucky sectors are (following any school), always observe these three golden rules:

- Never disturb or confront the Grand Duke Jupiter (e.g. sit facing his direction!)
- Never disturb the Place of the Three Killings; leave it alone.
- Never disturb the Deadly Five Yellow area; do not sleep or eat there or energize it.

Above: Be aware of the flying star feng shui taboos yearly and make sure you do not sit or eat there.

In the year:

YEAR	The ANIMAL SIGN or earthly branch is:	The Place of the Deadly Five Yellow (90 degrees) is:	The Place of the Three Killings (45 degrees) is:	The Grand Duke Jupiter's direction (it occupies only 15 degrees) is:
1999	RABBIT	SOUTH	WEST	EAST
2000	DRAGON	NORTH	SOUTH	EAST-SOUTH-EAST
2001	SNAKE	SOUTH-WEST	EAST	SOUTH-SOUTH-EAST
2002	HORSE	EAST	NORTH	SOUTH
2003	SHEEP	SOUTH-EAST	WEST	SOUTH-SOUTH-WEST
2004	MONKEY	CENTER	SOUTH	WEST-SOUTH-WEST
2005	ROOSTER	NORTH-WEST	EAST	WEST
2006	DOG	WEST	NORTH	WEST-NORTH-WEST
2007	BOAR	NORTH-EAST	WEST	NORTH-NORTH-WEST
2008	RAT	SOUTH	SOUTH	NORTH
2009	OX	NORTH	EAST	NORTH-NORTH-EAST
2010	TIGER	SOUTH-WEST	NORTH	EAST-NORTH-EAST

This is a very valuable table; study it carefully.

The four compatible astrological groupings

According to Chinese astrology, there are four groupings of compatibility, which comprises people born under three animal signs. People in a compatible group are believed to exhibit generally similar characteristics. They therefore tend to think alike and so get along with each other. They may not necessarily do things the same way, nor have the same energy patterns, courage and self-confidence, but, because their thought processes are similar, they tend to agree, and are said to be supportive of and good for each other. They may have different natures, but their actions generally complement and bring out the best in the others of their group. Pairings, partnerships and marriages between those born under animal signs within any of these triangles of affinities have a better-than-even chance of success. The four triangles of affinities are summarized below.

THE COMPETITORS:
The Rat, the Monkey and the Dragon
These are all action-oriented, highly competitive, positive and determined individuals. The Rat is massively insecure, requiring the Dragon's courage and supreme self-confidence. The Dragon is headstrong, and needs the craftiness of the Monkey or the Rat's astute eye for opportunity. The Monkey is fuelled by the Dragon's enthusiasm, and buoyed by the Rat's intelligence.

THE INTELLECTUALS:
The Snake, the Rooster and the Ox
These are the thinkers, visionaries and pragmatists of the Zodiac. They are purposeful, confident, resolute, tenacious, unwavering, and generally have formidable capabilities, as well as strong personalities. The Ox is rock solid and stable, but will benefit equally from the Snake's charm and smooth diplomacy or the Rooster's flamboyance. The Snake is crafty and ambitious, but will go further if helped by the Ox or the Rooster, and the Rooster's forthrightness will be tempered by the seductive Snake or the stable Ox.

THE INDEPENDENTS:
The Horse, the Dog and the Tiger
These are the free spirits of the Zodiac – emotional, subjective, highly principled, impetuous and restless. The Horse is the strategist, but he needs the Tiger's impulse to get started, or the Dog's determination to see things through. The Tiger's ferocity needs to be tempered by the Dog's good nature, while the Horse's restless spirit requires an outlet that the Tiger provides, or the calming influence that the Dog can give.

THE DIPLOMATS:
The Rabbit, the Sheep and the Boar
These are co-operative, soft-sell, low-profile people. They usually tend to be sensitive, sympathetic, sociable and eager-to-please. They are not risk-takers, nor are they madly intellectual or crafty. They provide each other with tender, loving care. The Rabbit's astuteness safeguards the Sheep's generosity, while the Sheep benefits from the Rabbit's sense of priorities. The Boar's strength complements the Rabbit's strategic thinking and the Sheep's more gentle approach.

81 How to bring love-luck to Rat people

The first sign of the Chinese Zodiac is the Rat, whose natural element is water. The "hour" of the Rat is between 11.00 p.m. and 1.00 a.m. Anyone born at midnight is said to be born in the hour of the Rat.

The compass direction of the Rat is between 337.5 and 7.5 degrees. This falls in the direction of north and is shown above on the compass marked with the Rat.

This sector of the house, which occupies an angle of 30 degrees, is deemed to be extremely lucky for any of its inhabitants who were born in the years of the Rat. Some of these are listed above; however, they have not been adjusted to take account of the lunar New Year. So if you were born in any of them during the month of January, you may not belong to the Rat year but rather to the one prior to it – that of the Boar. Similarly, you could still be a Rat if you were born in the January of the following year. To check your date of birth against the lunar calendar, please refer to the 100-year lunar calendar at the front of this book.

To energize the luck of love and relationships, there are several symbolic things which those born in Rat years can do:

Place an image of the Rat in the sector of your house that lies between the degrees indicated above. This will strengthen your presence in your home – particularly your lucky corner. You can also place the image of a Dragon or a Monkey in the north.

You can activate this area with a water feature, since this is the intrinsic element of your animal sign. It could, however, bring quite bad luck if your sector (i.e., north) were afflicted – e.g., with a toilet or a kitchen placed there – since this would affect your personal sector negatively.

Because your animal sign is the Rat, two other sectors are considered excellent for you. These correspond to the animal years of the Dragon and the Monkey. The direction of the Dragon is east-south-east, and the direction of the Monkey is west-south-west.

A perfect match for spirited, distinguished Rats

With a Monkey for fun and games on a roller coaster ride:

These two highly compatible individuals will have a great time in each other's company. The Rat's shrewd nature will find ready sympathy and acceptance through the Monkey's equally audacious sense of fun. Wrapped in their own materialistic world, they share the same values and pursue the same ambitions. They will be mutually admiring of each other's guile and methods, and will enthusiastically applaud each other's accomplishments. Equally clever and similarly ingenious, they will work well together, furthering a match quite literally made in heaven. One will tolerate the other's foibles. They will share the same jokes, strive for the same goals and boost each other's confidence. Together, they will accomplish much!

The Rat's natural element is water, while the Monkey's natural element is metal. In the cycle of element relationships, metal is said to produce water. One, therefore, supports the other. In this relationship, it is the Monkey who supports the Rat. Indeed, the Rat is likely to exhaust the Monkey! But, because they have a natural liking for each other, the Monkey will be willing to play this role, and he/she will do much to bolster the Rat's flagging confidence and insecurities. In other words, the Monkey will give strength to the Rat. In this pairing, either party can be of either sex for things to work. A pairing between a metal Rat and an earth Monkey introduces the additional elements of metal for the Rat (excellent) and earth for the Monkey (not so good). A metal Monkey and a water Rat union is excellent; both the heavenly stems and the earthly branches of the two horoscopes match perfectly!

With a Dragon for an absolutely delicious marriage:

This union unites the vital energy of the Dragon with the resourcefulness of the Rat, each efficiently enhancing the other's strengths and capabilities. The Rat will admire and be drawn to the Dragon's dynamism, and will happily draw inspiration and strength from the Dragon's exuberance and enthusiasm, in the process assuaging his or her own insecurity. There will be trust and belief in each other, and neither will be jealous of the other. The Dragon is the "big picture" person – content to leave all the tedious details in the hands of the capable and ingenious Rat. At the same time, the Dragon's lack of guile will be more than made up for by the Rat's more crafty ways. Together, they make a truly handsome and magnificent pair.

The Rat's natural element is water, while the Dragon's is earth. In the cycle of element relationships, earth is said to control water, yet, together, earth and water provide the ingredients for plants to grow and thrive. In this relationship, therefore, it is the Dragon who will always have the upper hand, and, indeed, should be the more dominant partner. It is the Rat who must look up to the Dragon and cheer and encourage him or her on. Because they have a natural sympathy for each other, the Rat will be quite willing to play this more subservient role, and they will not experience fear that things will go wrong in the relationship.

Monkey years
1920
1932
1944
1956
1968
1980
1992
2004

Dragon Years
1916
1928
1940
1952
1964
1976
1988
2000

83 Enhancing the love life of Ox people

The Ox is the second sign of the Chinese Zodiac. Its intrinsic element is earth. The "hour" of the Ox is between 1.00 and 3.00 a.m. Anyone born between those hours is said to be born in the hour of the Ox.

The compass direction of the Ox is between 7.5 and 37.5 degrees. This falls in the direction of north-north-east and is shown on the compass right, marked with the Ox.

You will find that this sector of the house occupies an angle of 30 degrees. This part of a home is deemed to be very lucky for any of its residents who are born in the years of the Ox, some of which are listed above. However, they have not been adjusted to take account of the lunar New Year. So if you were born in any of the above years during, for instance, January, the chances are you do not belong to the Ox year but to the year prior to it – that of the Rat. Similarly, you could still be an Ox if you were born in the January of the following year. To check your date of birth against the lunar calendar, please refer to the 100-year lunar calendar at the front of this book.

Ox Years

1913
1925
1937
1949
1961
1973
1985
1997

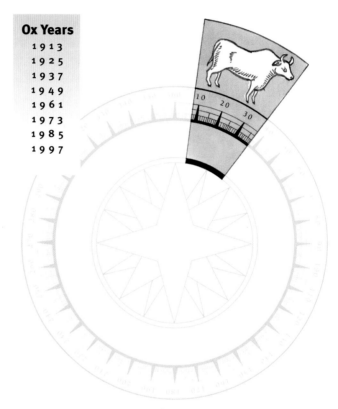

To attract the luck of relationships, love and family to the Ox sector of the home, there are several symbolic things you can do:

Place a symbolic wish-fulfilling cow in the Ox sector of your house. Use the image of a cow or a bull made of clay, crystal or some other material that is an earth element.

You can activate this area with any earth element feature, since this is the intrinsic element of your animal sign. In addition, introduce a bright light here.

Two other sectors are deemed to be excellent for the Ox. These correspond to the animal years of the Snake and Rooster. The direction of the Snake is south-south-east, and the Rooster's is west.

Love for the steely Miss Ox and strong Mr Ox

84

With a Snake for a deeply abiding love match:

This will be a mutually enhancing relationship. The powerful and dependable Ox is irresistibly drawn to the seductive and ambitious Snake, who in turn finds the Ox's strength comforting and attractive. Both will appreciate the synergy inherent in their union, and the support they give to each other will intensify the relationship as the years go by. In terms of control, the wily Snake exerts a greater influence over the Ox, but it will be the Ox who will publicly accomplish great things, although he/she will forever stay under the spell of the Snake. Theirs is a relationship that is immune to outside interference, and the commitment they give to each other will be strong and abiding. This will be a love-match that grows healthier with the passing years.

The Snake's natural element is fire, while the Ox's is earth. In the cycle of element relationships, fire produces earth. One, therefore, feeds the other. In this relationship, it is the Snake who supports the Ox. Indeed, the Ox could well exhaust the Snake, unless he/she receives an extra dose of fire, or is helped along by wood! Their natural affinity with each other makes the Snake quite willing to play second fiddle to the Ox. It will not be surprising for the Ox to totally adore the Snake in this union!

Above: A snake and an ox will have a great love match, while an ox and a rooster will make their marriage work.

Rooster Years
1921
1933
1945
1957
1969
1981
1993
2005

Snake Years
1917
1929
1941
1953
1965
1977
1989
2001

With a Rooster, a match made in heaven:

Such a sensible and supportive pair! Both individuals are practical, stoic, prepared to sacrifice for the greater good – and both are so ambitious and determined to make their marriage work! Theirs will be a home where everything runs like clockwork – where the efficient hand of the Rooster is clearly in evidence, and where the influence of the Ox's down-to-earth taste in furnishings and decor is everywhere in sight. The patient Ox puts up with the Rooster's tendency to take control and dominate, while the pragmatic Rooster appreciates the Ox's seemingly tedious prevarication. The Rooster understands the way the Ox's mind works, and accepts that the Ox cannot be rushed. Theirs is a long-term, successful commitment to each other.

The Ox's natural element is earth, while the Rooster's is metal. In the cycle of element relationships, earth produces metal. One party, therefore, clearly supports the other, and here it is the Ox who supports the Rooster. Their natural affinity, however, makes the Ox more than happy to do so, and the Rooster enjoys the role of the taker in this alliance. Indeed, the Ox is likely to hero-worship the high-flying Rooster!

85 Enhancing the love life of Tiger people

The Tiger is the third sign of the Chinese Zodiac. Its natural element is wood. The "hour" of the Tiger is between 3.00 and 5.00 a.m. Anyone born between those hours is said to be born in the hour of the Tiger.

The compass direction of the Tiger is between 37.5 and 67.5 degrees. This falls in the direction of east-north-east, shown on the compass right, marked with the Tiger.

This segment of a house, which corresponds to the 30 degrees indicated above, is the Tiger's auspicious sector. It is considered very lucky for any of its residents born in the years of the Tiger. These years are listed here. However, these years have not been adjusted to take account of the lunar New Year. Therefore, if you were born in any of these years during January, you probably do not belong to the Tiger year, but to the year prior to it, which is that of the Ox. Similarly, you could still be a Tiger if you were born in the January of the following year. To check your date of birth against the lunar calendar, please refer to the 100-year lunar calendar at the front of this book.

To energize auspicious romance and love luck in your personal earthly branch sector, those born in the years of the Tiger can do the following:

Place decorative Tiger images in the sector of your house situated between the degrees indicated above. As a Tiger person, you will gain from the chi created by Tiger images, whether these are ceramic decorative pieces or in paintings. Wooden sculptures of the Tiger would be excellent, as they energize the natural wood element and are beneficial. Metal windchimes placed here harm you.

You can energize this sector with any wood element feature, since this is the inherent element of your animal sign. It will, however, bring bad luck if your sector (i.e., east-north-east) is afflicted with a toilet or a kitchen placed there, since this would affect your personal sector negatively.

Two other sectors deemed to be excellent for Tigers are those that correspond to the animal years of the Horse and Dog. The Horse's direction is south, and the Dog's is west-north-west.

Tiger Years
1914
1926
1938
1950
1962
1974
1986
1998

Partners for the mesmerizing Tigers

Can find love with a Horse – for an auspicious and volcanic passion:

These two are kindred spirits! Their impulsive, restless, energetic natures gel perfectly, and they have a deep, perfect understanding of the other's temperament. They will fight and argue, then make up with intense good humour. These are two fiery and volatile temperaments. They are equally happy travelling through the Sahara Desert or climbing in the mountains of Nepal.

Both are free spirits, unshackled by anything conventional and their individual courage complements the other's. They will share great adventures. In their life together, they are both magnificent risk-takers, and, in love, they share a passion only they can understand. This is a high-voltage relationship.

The Horse's natural element is fire, while the Tiger's is wood. In the cycle of element relationships, wood produces fire. One party clearly supports the other, and, in this case, it is the Tiger who supports the Horse, and who will bring substance and sustenance to the relationship. The natural affinity between the two fuels the Tiger's enthusiasm, thereby increasing his productivity and strengthening his resolve.

With a Dog, life is perfect:

Here we are talking about a totally adorable Dog and an equally engaging Tiger! Both have volatile tempers and can grow very angry, but their natural affinity becomes evident when together, and, although they may become annoyed with each other, they never stay so for long. The Dog understands the Tiger's impetuous nature completely, and is happy to be

Horse Years
1918
1930
1942
1954
1966
1978
1990
2002

Dog Years
1922
1934
1946
1958
1970
1982
1994
2006

indulgent. The Tiger, meanwhile, comprehends the Dog's altruistic and cautious nature, and does not resent being reined in occasionally. There is a great deal of mutual respect in this relationship, and the normally ferocious Tiger becomes a pussycat when partnered with the Dog. It is a truly affectionate match!

The Dog's natural element is earth, while the Tiger's is wood. In the cycle of element relationships, wood controls earth. One party is, therefore, clearly dominant, and in this case it is the Tiger who dominates and is always in control. But the Dog does not mind this situation. Their natural affinity softens the Tiger's touch, and the Dog is content to let the Tiger be in charge.

87 Enhancing the love life of Rabbit people

The Rabbit is the fourth sign of the Chinese Zodiac. Its intrinsic element is wood. The "hour" of the Rabbit is said to be between 5.00 and 7.00 a.m. Anyone who is born between those hours is said to be born in the hour of the Rabbit.

The compass direction of the Rabbit is between 67.5 and 97.5 degrees. This falls in the direction of east, which is shown on the compass right, marked with the Rabbit.

You will find this sector of the house, which occupies an angle of 30 degrees, is very lucky for any of its residents who were born in the years of the Rabbit, some of which are listed here. However, these years have not been adjusted to take account of the lunar New Year. Therefore, if you were born in any Rabbit year during January, you probably do not belong to the Rabbit year, but to the year prior to it, which is that of the Tiger. Also, you could still be a Rabbit if you were born in the January of the following year. To check your date of birth against the lunar calendar, please refer to the 100-year lunar calendar at the front of this book.

To energize good love luck in your personal earthly branch sector, there are several symbolic things you can do:

Place images of the Rabbit in the sector of your house that occupies the area between the degrees indicated above. To enhance the area's intrinsic energy, display wooden carvings or sculptures of rabbits – always in pairs, and never alone!

You can activate the same sector with any wood element feature, as this is the intrinsic element of your animal sign. If this eastern

Rabbit Years
1915
1927
1939
1951
1963
1975
1987
1999

sector contains a toilet or a kitchen, however, it will bring bad luck for you, since this will affect your personal sector negatively.

Two other sectors deemed to be excellent for Rabbits are those that correspond to the animal years of the Sheep and Boar. The Sheep's direction is south-south-west and the Boar's is north-north-west.

The virtuous Rabbit woman and the amiable man

Can find love with the Sheep – a wobbly start, but a solid relationship:

This is a partnership between two beautifully matched individuals who make fantastic music together. The normally secretive Sheep will open his or her heart to the astute and diplomatic Rabbit, and the Rabbit will skilfully draw out all of the Sheep's latent and hidden talents with a combination of tender care and genuine love. A blend of encouragement with outstanding motivational skills, on the Rabbit's part, brings forth all that is best in the Sheep. As a team, therefore, these two work well together and achieve much, building a comfortable and loving home. In terms of temperament, the Rabbit is able to soothe and comfort the Sheep's tendencies towards despondency and depression, in the process injecting tremendous zeal and confidence into his/her mate. A truly great match!

The Sheep's natural element is earth, while the Rabbit's is wood. In the cycle of element relationships, wood controls earth. One party is clearly in control, and, in this case, it is the Rabbit who dominates the relationship. This augurs well for the alliance, because the Rabbit brings out the best in the Sheep, and, although he/she is in control, it is a self-effacing control that is couched in subtlety, as the Rabbit is happy to stay behind the scenes.

Sheep Years
1919
1931
1943
1955
1967
1979
1991
2003

Boar Years
1923
1935
1947
1959
1971
1983
1995
2007

Below: A Rabbit and Sheep are perfect; with a Boar – a good mix.

Love with a Boar – almost custom-made for each other:

In many ways, this is a case of opposites attracting – the Boar being loud and somewhat aggressive, and the Rabbit quieter and subtler. The Boar utilizes strength and stamina, while the Rabbit uses his/her innate intelligence to think carefully through problems. Yet the two seem to think alike, and they want the same things in life. Where they differ is the way they go about achieving their goals. When the two come together, it is like a blending of two complementary halves. Their natural affinity makes them like each other from the beginning, and, when they start discovering each other's talents, the two get along like a house on fire. They make a great team because, while the Rabbit is happy to manipulate things from behind the scenes, the Boar does not mind being in the spotlight. Each brings out the best in the other, and, when either one stumbles, the other will always be around to give a helping hand, and a broad strong shoulder.

The Boar's natural element is water, while the Rabbit's is wood. In the cycle of element relationships, water produces wood. One party clearly provides the sustenance and support here, and it is the Boar, who is considered to be excellent good fortune for the Rabbit! This augurs well for the alliance.

89

Enhancing the love life of Dragon people

The Dragon is the fifth sign of the Chinese Zodiac. Its intrinsic element is earth. The "hour" of the Dragon is said to be between 7.00 and 9.00 a.m. Anyone born between those hours is said to be born in the hour of the Dragon.

The compass direction of the Dragon is between 97.5 and 127.5 degrees. This falls in the direction of the east-south-east and is shown on the compass below, marked with the Dragon.

This sector occupies an angle of 30 degrees and is said to be the most lucky part of the house for any of its inhabitants who were born in the years of the Dragon, some of which are listed above. However, they have not been adjusted to take account of the lunar New Year. Thus, if you were born in any of them during January, you may not belong to the Dragon year, but to the year prior to it – that of the Rabbit. Also, you could still be a Dragon if you were born in the January of the following year. To check your date of birth against the lunar calendar, please refer to the 100-year lunar calendar situated at the front of this book.

To energize good love luck in your personal earthly branch sector, there are things you can do to energize the symbolism of your animal sign:

Place images of the Dragon in the section of your house that lies between the degrees indicated above. To enhance this area's intrinsic energy, display dragons made of earth materials – like clay, porcelain, crystal, etc. – or hang a dragon painting here.

You can activate this sector with any earth element feature, as this is the intrinsic element

Dragon Years
1916
1928
1940
1952
1964
1976
1988
2000

of your animal sign. This will, however, bring bad luck for you if the east-south-east contains a toilet or kitchen, since this will create afflictions or problems for you.

Two other sectors that are deemed to be excellent for those born in Dragon years are those which correspond to the Monkey and Rat animal years. The Monkey's direction is west-south-west and the Rat's is north.

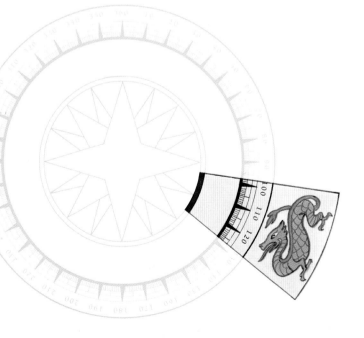

The charismatic lady and impetuous male Dragon

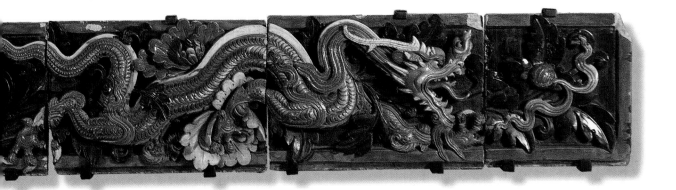

Can find love with the Monkey – and bring out the best in each other:

Here are two high-performers whose combined energy and resolute determination are simply hard to beat. The Dragon's grand plans find ready acceptance and support from the ambitious Monkey. When things go wrong, as they invariably will, the Monkey's guile and shrewdness will invent solutions for getting them both out of their tight spot. The Dragon admires the Monkey's ingenuity – nay, is mesmerized by it – while the Monkey ardently admires the Dragon's courage and strength. Together, this pair is not to be trifled with, especially since their natural affinity makes them natural allies. In business, they bring out the best in each other. In love, they inspire and excite each other. Potentially they are an unbeatable match.

The Dragon's natural element is earth, while the Monkey's is metal. In the cycle of element relationships, earth produces metal. One, therefore, supports the other. In this relationship, it is the Dragon who supports the Monkey. Indeed, the Monkey could well exhaust the Dragon, unless he is reinforced by extra earth or helped by fire! Together they have a natural affinity.

A soul mate for the Dragon: the Rat, for a wonderful marriage:

The Dragon's vital energy unites brilliantly with the resourcefulness of the Rat. One will magnify the other's potency and substance. The Rat is bowled over by the Dragon's charisma, enthusiasm and accompanying exuberance. He or she finds comfort in the Dragon's loudness, and in the process assuages his or her own insecurities. Both respect each other. The Dragon is a "big picture" person, content to leave details to the capable and ingenious Rat. The Dragon's lack of guile is complemented by the Rat's more calculating ways. Together, they are magnificent.

The Rat's natural element is water, while the Dragon's is earth. In the cycle of element relationships, earth is said to control water, but, together, earth and water help plants grow. So it is the Dragon who has the upper hand, and will be dominant. It is the Rat who will cheer him or her on. They will experience no fear of things going wrong.

Monkey Years

1920
1932
1944
1956
1968
1980
1992
2004

Rat Years

1912
1924
1936
1948
1960
1972
1984
1996

91

Enhancing the love life of Snake people

The Snake is the sixth sign of the Chinese Zodiac. Its intrinsic element is fire. The "hour" of the Snake is between 9.00 and 11.00 a.m. Anyone born between these hours is said to be born in the hour of the Snake.

The compass direction of the Snake is between 127.5 and 157.5 degrees. This falls in the direction of east-south-east, shown on the compass below, marked with the Snake. This sector of the house, which occupies an angle of 30 degrees, is deemed to be most lucky for

any of its inhabitants who were born in the years of the Snake, some of which are listed left. These years have not been adjusted to take account of the lunar New Year. So if you were born in any of these years during, for instance, January, you may not belong to the Snake year, but to the year prior to it, which is that of the Dragon. Similarly, you could still be a Snake if you were born in the January of the following year. To check your date of birth against the lunar calendar, please refer to the 100-year lunar calendar at the front of this book.

To energize good love luck in your personal earthly branch sector, there are several symbolic things you might consider doing:

Place images of the Snake in the sector of your house that are situated between the degrees indicated above. In order to enhance this site's intrinsic energy, display the Snake image in a red colour – preferably one made of wood, since wood produces fire!

You can activate this area with any fire element feature, since this is the intrinsic element of your animal sign. So, keep this sector brightly lit! However, this will bring bad luck for you if this south-south-east sector contains a toilet or kitchen, as this will affect your personal sector negatively.

For those born in Snake years, sectors which correspond favourably with the Rooster and Ox are also deemed excellent for them. The direction of the Rooster is west and the direction of the Ox is north-north-east.

The tantalizing lady and seductive Snake man

Below: A Rooster and Snake can be a powerful love match, while an Ox and Snake can have an enduring relationship.

Can find love with a Rooster – whose eyes will be only for each other:

These two think alike, have similar tastes, and simply adore each other. In this relationship, the Snake is the planner, the strategist and the one with the eye for the main chance. But it will be the Rooster who has the tenacity, decisiveness and skills to take productive action. Together, they make a powerful pair. The Rooster will listen to and admire the Snake's ingenious schemes, and, with characteristic efficiency and hard work, will transform all of their grand plans into reality. Both have formidable intellects, and, while the Snake is intuitive, the Rooster is practical. In business, they are hard to beat. In love, they stay devoted and true to each other – a very passionate pair indeed!

The Snake's natural element is fire, while the Rooster's is metal. In the cycle of element relationships, fire controls metal. One party is, therefore, clearly dominant. In this case, it is the Snake who dominates the Rooster. Their natural sympathy for each other, however, makes the Rooster more than willing to bow to the Snake's clearly more superior role. It will not be at all surprising for the Rooster to totally succumb to the Snake's considerable charms!

Love with the Ox – a deeply abiding love-match:

With the Ox, the Snake finds a mutually rewarding relationship. The forceful and reliable Ox is irresistibly drawn to the beguiling and resourceful Snake, who in turn finds the Ox's intensity very attractive indeed. Both appreciate the synergy inherent in their union, and the support they give to each other will strengthen their relationship as the years go by. In terms of disposition, the artful Snake exerts a greater influence over the Ox, but it is the Ox who will accomplish great things, being the more determined of the two. The relationship between them is strong and will endure. If neither allows outsiders to interfere, this is a love-match that becomes stronger as the years go on.

The Snake's natural element is fire, while the Ox's is earth. In the cycle of element relationships, fire produces earth. One, therefore, feeds the other. In this relationship, it is the Snake who supports the Ox. Indeed, the Ox could well exhaust the Snake unless he/she receives an extra dose of fire, or is helped along by wood! Their natural sympathy for each other makes the Snake very willing to play second fiddle to the Ox. It will not be at all surprising for the Ox to totally adore the Snake in this combination!

93 Enhancing the love life of Horse people

The Horse is the seventh sign of the Chinese Zodiac. Its intrinsic element is fire. The "hour" of the Horse is said to be between 11.00 a.m. and 1.00 p.m. Anyone born between those hours is said to be born in the hour of the Horse.

The compass direction of the sign of the Horse is between 157.5 and 187.5 degrees. This falls in the direction of the south and is shown on the compass below, marked with the symbol of the Horse.

This sector of the house, which occupies an angle of 30 degrees, is very lucky for any of its inhabitants who were born in the years of the Horse, some of which are listed right. However, they have not been adjusted to take account of the lunar New Year. Therefore, if you were born in any of these years during January, for example, it is probable that you do not belong to a Horse year, but to the year before it, which is that of the Snake. Similarly, you could still be deemed a Horse if you were born in the January of the following year. To check your date of birth, refer to the lunar calendar at the front of this book.

Horse years
1918
1930
1942
1954
1966
1978
1990
2002

To energize, and therefore maximize, love and wealth luck in your personal earthly branch sector, there are several symbolic things that you can do:

Place images of the Horse in the sector of your house that lies between the degrees indicated here. To enhance the area's intrinsic energy, display the Horse image in whites and reds – these are yang colours. Also, choose images that are made of wood, as this is the element that produces fire!

You can activate this sector with any fire element feature, since this is the intrinsic element of your animal sign. So keep this section brightly lit! It will be bad luck for you if this area (i.e., the south) contains a toilet or kitchen, since this would damage your personal sector seriously.

For those who were born in Horse years, sectors that correspond to the animal years of the Dog and the Tiger are also deemed to be excellent. The direction of the Dog is west-north-west, and the direction of the Tiger is east-north-east.

The warm lady and the headstrong Horse man

Can find an endearing match with a Dog:

These two signs have perfectly compatible temperaments. Theirs is a peaceful home, where there is a noticeable absence of fireworks and bad temper. They give in to each other most of the time, both being sensible and rational human beings. There is generally co-operation and communication between them, and even when the Horse occasionally grows restive, it does not affect the relationship adversely, because the Dog is prepared to listen and is able to understand. Neither will attempt to dominate or compete with the other, and their natural affinity makes them trust each other implicitly.

At work, the Horse will be the more aggressive of the two, and the Dog is happy to let the Horse take the lead. In love, the two will be really devoted to each other – being neither possessive nor interfering with each other.

Tiger Years
1914
1926
1938
1950
1962
1974
1986
1998

Dog Years
1922
1934
1946
1958
1970
1982
1994
2006

The Dog's natural element is earth, while the Horse's element is fire. In the cycle of element relationships, fire produces earth. One party is, therefore, clearly supportive of the other, and, in this case, it is the Horse who supports and provides for the Dog. Their natural sympathy for each other, however, makes the restless and headstrong Horse more than happy to do the giving, while the Dog happily sits back and really enjoys all of the Horse's loving generosity!

Love with the Tiger – a match with passion:

The two kindred spirits of the Horse and the Tiger are naturally drawn together by their impulsive, restless and energetic natures. They develop a deep and consummate passion for each other, and their temperaments gel perfectly, despite being fiery and volatile. Their sense of adventure fuels great plans, and they are equally happy skiing at the South Pole or scuba-diving in the Maldives. Both are free spirits, unshackled from anything conventional, and their individual courage and respect are a source of attraction and electricity between them. They will share great adventures. In business, they are both magnificent risk-takers, and, in love, they share a passion that only they can understand. This is potentially an electric relationship.

The Horse's natural element is fire, while the Tiger's is wood. In the cycle of element relationships, wood produces fire. One party clearly supports the other, and, in this case, it is the Tiger who supports the Horse, and who will bring substance and sustenance to the relationship. Their natural affinity fuels the Tiger's enthusiasm, thereby increasing his productivity and strengthening his resolve.

95

Enhancing the love life of Sheep people

The Sheep is the eighth sign of the Chinese Zodiac. Its intrinsic element is earth. The "hour" of the Sheep is said to be between 1.00 and 3.00 p.m. Anyone born between those hours is said to be born in the hour of the Sheep.

The compass direction of the Sheep is between 187.5 and 217.5 degrees. This falls in the direction of the south-south-west and is shown on the compass below, marked with the Sheep.

This sector of the house, which occupies an angle of 30 degrees, is very lucky for any of its inhabitants who were born in the Sheep years, some of which are listed above. These years have not been adjusted to accommodate the lunar New Year. So if you were born in any of the above years during January, you may not belong to the Sheep year, but to the year prior to it, which is the year of the Horse.

Similarly, you could still be a Sheep year person if you were born in the January of the following year. To check your date of birth against the lunar calendar, please refer to the 100-year lunar calendar which appears at the front of this book.

In order to energize good love luck into your personal earthly branch sector, there are several symbolic things you can do:

Place images of the Sheep or Goat in the sector of your house that lies between the degrees indicated here. To enhance the area's intrinsic energy, display the Sheep or Goat images in earth element materials.

You can activate this space with the fire element, since fire produces earth. The sector will also benefit from porcelain and other decorative ceramic ware.

For those born in Sheep years, there are two other sectors that are also deemed to be most excellent. These correspond to the years of the Boar and Rabbit. The Boar's section is identified with north-north-west, and the Rabbit's with east.

Sheep Years

1919
1931
1943
1955
1967
1979
1991
2003

The gentle lady and the romantic male Sheep

Can find love with the Boar – a happy, mellow and smooth affair:

This has to be one of the sweetest pairings in the Chinese horoscope. The natural affinity between the Sheep and the Boar is reflected in their genuine concern for and patience with each other. The sensitive Sheep nature finds sustenance, comfort and love from the Boar, whose broad shoulders willingly enfold the Sheep in a warm cocoon of love. Nor is the Sheep merely a love object; indeed, the two find pleasure in working and planning their life together. The earthy Boar admires the Sheep's gentle, classy disposition. Both have healthy appetites and are equally generous. In love, they enjoy simple pleasures, with neither going off on a tangent or succumbing to outside distractions. Loyalty features prominently in this relationship, and it is one of the most compatible of horoscope pairings.

The Sheep's natural element is earth, while the Boar's is water. In the cycle of element relationships, earth controls water. One party is clearly in control, and, in this case, it is the Sheep who dominates the relationship. Their natural affinity smoothes interactions between them, and the more aggressive Boar gives in easily to the subtle and understated Sheep. That it is the Sheep who will dominate this relationship is not surprising, since the Boar is neither as clever nor as worldly wise as the Sheep. Indeed, in this union, it is the Sheep who steers the Boar out of dangerous waters, and the latter accepts it with good grace!

In love, the Rabbit and Sheep make fantastic music together:

This pair make sweet music together! The usually reticent Sheep will open his or her heart to the perceptive and highly sensitive Rabbit, who will ingeniously draw out all of the Sheep's inherent needs with tender and genuine love. A combination of encouragement and charm draws out all that is best in the Sheep. As a couple, these two enjoy their time together, and they achieve much, both as partners and later while building a family together. In terms of temperament, the Rabbit soothes and comforts the Sheep's tendencies towards depression, in the process giving tremendous zeal and confidence to his/her mate – truly a great match.

The Sheep's natural element is earth while the Rabbit's is wood. In the cycle of element relationships, wood controls earth. One party is clearly in control, and, in this case, it is the Rabbit who dominates the relationship. This augurs well for the alliance, because the Rabbit brings out the best in the Sheep, and, although he/she is in control, it is a self-effacing control that is couched in subtlety, as the Rabbit is happy to stay behind the scenes.

Above: A Sheep and a Boar can have a loyal and warm relationship, while a Sheep and Rabbit can experience true and tender love.

Boar Years
1923
1935
1947
1959
1971
1983
1995
2007

Rabbit Years
1915
1927
1939
1951
1963
1975
1987
1999

97

Enhancing the love life of Monkey people

Monkey Years
1920
1932
1944
1956
1968
1980
1992
2004

The Monkey is the ninth sign of the Chinese Zodiac. Its intrinsic element is metal. The "hour" of the Monkey is said to be between 3.00 and 5.00 p.m. Anyone born between those hours is said to be born in the hour of the Monkey.

The compass direction of the Monkey is between 217.5 and 247.5 degrees. This falls in the direction of the west-south-west, and is shown on the compass below, marked with the Monkey.

This sector of the house, which occupies an angle of 30 degrees, is deemed to be very lucky for those residents born in any of the years of the Monkey, some of which are listed above. These years have not been adjusted to take account of the lunar New Year. So, if you were born in any of the above years during January, for instance, you may not belong to the Monkey year, but to the year prior to it, which is that of the Sheep. Similarly, you could still be a Monkey year person if you were born in the January of the following year. To check

your date of birth against the lunar calendar, please refer to the 100-year lunar calendar at the front of this book.

To energize good love luck in your personal earthly branch sector, there are several symbolic things you can do:

Place images of the Monkey in the part of your house that lies between the degrees indicated left. To enhance the area's intrinsic energy, display a painting of a monkey with peaches; this is a particularly auspicious image when painted on clay or porcelain.

You can activate this space with any metal element feature, since this is the intrinsic element of your animal sign. So, bells and wind chimes are suitable there. However, it will bring bad luck for you if a toilet or kitchen is located in this area (i.e., the west-south-west); this would affect your personal sector badly.

Those born in Monkey years will also benefit from good symbols placed in areas corresponding to Rat and Dragon years. The sector of the Rat is north, and that of the Dragon is east-south-east.

The charming lady and impudent male Monkey

Above: The Monkey and the Rat can make a heavenly match, while the Monkey and the Dragon can have an exciting, inspirational relationship.

Love with the Rat brings a roaring good time:

The Monkey's audacious sense of fun finds a kindred spirit in the Rat's natural predilection for having a good time. Both are wrapped deliciously in their own materialistic worlds. They share the same values and pursue the same ambitions. They will be mutually admiring of each other's guile and methods, and will enthusiastically applaud each other's accomplishments. Equally clever and similarly ingenious, they will work well together, furthering a match quite literally made in heaven. Each will tolerate the other's foibles, social ambitions and penchant for parties. They will share the same jokes, strive for the same goals and boost each other's confidence. Together, they can accomplish much! Danger comes only when the fun and games run out.

The Rat's natural element is water while the Monkey's is metal. In the cycle of element relationships, metal is said to produce water. One, therefore, supports the other. In this relationship, the Monkey supports the Rat. Indeed, the Rat will be likely to exhaust the Monkey! But, because they have a natural affinity together, the Monkey will be willing to play this role, and he/she will do much to bolster the Rat's flagging confidence and insecurities. In other words, the Monkey will give strength to the Rat. In this pairing, either party can be of either sex for things to work well.

Rat Years
1912
1924
1936
1948
1960
1972
1984
1996

Dragon Years
1916
1928
1940
1952
1964
1976
1988
2000

Love with the Dragon is a match of high performers:

Make no doubt about it, these two are high performers whose combined determination and ambitions are hard to beat. The Dragon's grand blueprints for success find ready acceptance from the resourceful Monkey and, when things go wrong, as they occasionally will, the Monkey's shrewdness and the Dragon's never-flagging optimism see them through. The Dragon admires the Monkey's creativity and is mesmerized by it, while the Monkey ardently admires the Dragon's enthusiasm and positive attitude towards everything. Together, they can seem like a formidable pair 'not to be trifled with. Their affinity makes them natural allies. In business, their team-work and co-operation bring out the best in both of them. In love, they will inspire and excite each other.

The Dragon's natural element is earth while the Monkey's is metal. In the cycle of element relationships, earth produces metal. One, therefore, supports the other. In this relationship, it is the Dragon who supports the Monkey. Indeed, the Monkey could well exhaust the Dragon, unless he receives extra doses of earth, or is helped along by fire! Their natural compatibility makes the Dragon willing to play second fiddle to the Monkey. It will not be at all surprising for the Dragon to really adore the Monkey in this union!

99 Enhancing the love life of Rooster people

Rooster Years

1921
1933
1945
1957
1969
1981
1993
2005

the year prior to it, which is that of the Monkey. Similarly, you could still be a Rooster if you were born in the January of the following year. To check your date of birth against the lunar calendar, please refer to the 100-year lunar calendar which is at the front of this book.

To energize good love luck in your personal earthly branch sector, there are several symbolic things you can do:

Place images of the Rooster in the part of your house which falls between the degrees indicated here. To enhance the intrinsic energy of this animal, you should display Rooster images and sculptures that are made either from clay or from porcelain.

The Rooster is the tenth sign of the Chinese Zodiac. Its intrinsic element is metal. The "hour" of the Rooster is said to be between 5.00 and 7.00 p.m. Anyone born between those hours is said to be born in the hour of the Rooster.

The compass direction of the Rooster is between 247.5 and 277.5 degrees. This falls in the direction of west shown on the compass above, marked with the Rooster.

This sector of the house, which occupies an angle of 30 degrees, is deemed to be very lucky for any of its residents who were born in the years of the Rooster, some of which are listed above. However, they have not been adjusted to take account of the lunar New Year. So if you were born in any of the above years, for instance, during January, chances are that you do not belong to the Rooster year, but to

Activate this area with the metal element, because this is the intrinsic element of your animal sign. So, bells and wind chimes are fine to use as enhancements within this space. However, it will bring bad luck for you if this sector (i.e., the west) is afflicted by a toilet or a kitchen placed there, as this would cause your personal sector to be badly affected.

Rooster year people also benefit from sectors that correspond to the animal years of the Snake and the Ox. The direction of the Snake is south-south-east, and that of the Ox is north-north-east.

The resourceful Rooster lady and the resilient male

Can find such compatibility with the Snake that it hurts!

These two think alike, have the same tastes, and simply adore each other. In this relationship, the Snake plans and the Rooster executes. The Snake is the strategist, the one with an eye for opportunity, but it is the Rooster who boldly moves forward. In their love relationship, it is the Rooster who decisively takes control. Together, they make a powerful pair. The Rooster admires the Snake's ingenious schemes, regarding them as both brilliant and creative, and, with characteristic efficiency and hard work, will transform ideas and suggestions into a reality which they can both relish. They each have formidable intellects; but the Snake is intuitive and the Rooster practical. In business, they are hard to beat. In love, they stay devoted and true to each other – making a very passionate pair indeed!

The Snake's natural element is fire, while the Rooster's element is metal. In the cycle of element relationships, fire controls metal. One party is, therefore, more dominant. In the case of theses two, it is the Snake who dominates over the Rooster. However, their natural compatibility makes the Rooster more than willing to bow to the Snake's more superior role in the relationship. It is not at all surprising when the Rooster totally succumbs to the Snake's considerable charms!

Love with the Ox – two strong individuals in an intense match:

These are two individuals who are practical, stoic and prepared to sacrifice for the greater good. The intensity between these two is mesmerizing to watch because both are so controlled. They are ambitious and determined individuals who will work hard to produce a brilliant marriage. Theirs will be a home or a business where everything runs like clockwork – where the efficient hand of the Rooster is clearly in evidence, and the influence of the Ox's down-to-earth taste in furnishings and decor is everywhere in sight. The patient Ox puts up with the Rooster's tendency to take control and be dominant, and the pragmatic Rooster appreciates the Ox's seemingly tedious prevarication. Underneath all the efficiency, however, is a genuine true love and passion. Theirs is a long-term and successful commitment to each other.

The Ox's natural element is earth, while the Rooster's is metal. In the cycle of element relationships, earth produces metal. One party is, therefore, clearly supportive of the other, and, in this case, it is the Ox who supports and provides for the Rooster. Their natural affinity, however, makes the Ox more than happy to do so, and the Rooster clearly enjoys the role of the taker. Indeed, the Ox is likely to hero-worship the high-flying Rooster.

Snake Years
1917
1929
1941
1953
1965
1977
1989
2001

Ox Years
1913
1925
1937
1949
1961
1973
1985
1997

101 Enhancing the love life of Dog people

The Dog is the eleventh sign of the Chinese Zodiac. Its intrinsic element is metal. The "hour" of the Dog is said to be between 5.00 and 7.00 p.m. Anyone who is born between those hours is said to be born in the hour of the Dog.

The compass direction of the Dog is between 277.5 and 307.5 degrees. This falls in the direction of the west and is shown on the compass above, marked with the Dog.

This sector of the house, which occupies an angle of 30 degrees, is deemed to be very lucky for any of its residents who were born in the years of the Dog, some of which are listed above. These years have not been adjusted to take account of the lunar New Year. So if you were born in any of the above years during, for example, January, you may well not belong to the Dog year, but to the preceding year – that of the Rooster. Similarly, you could still be a Dog if you were born in the January of the following year. To check your date of birth against the lunar calendar, please refer to the 100-year lunar calendar at the front of this book.

To energize good love luck in your personal earthly branch sector, there are several symbolic things you can do:

Place images of the Dog in the sector of your house that falls between the degrees indicated above. To enhance this area's intrinsic energy, display Dog images and sculptures that are made of ceramics or porcelain.

You can activate this space with the metal element, as this is the intrinsic element of your animal sign. So, bells and wind chimes are fine to place here. However, these will bring bad luck for you if this sector (i.e., the west-north-west) is afflicted with a toilet or a kitchen placed there, since this would affect your personal sector badly.

Dog year people also benefit from sectors corresponding to the animal years of the Tiger and the Horse. The direction of the Tiger is east-north-east, and the direction of the Horse is south.

The generous Dog lady and the loyal male Dog

When in love with the Tiger, a natural affinity shines forth:

These two potentially have volatile tempers, but their instinctive natural affinity quells all thoughts of anger. Compatibility between them will be very strong, and shines forth when they are together. The Dog is enthralled by the Tiger's impetuosity, and finds it natural to be tolerant and indulgent. The Tiger understands the Dog's altruistic, cautious nature and does not resent being reined in occasionally. Indeed, there is so much love and mutual respect in this relationship that the ferocious Tiger becomes a pussycat with the Dog – a really adorable match!

The Dog's natural element is earth, while the Tiger's is wood. In the cycle of element relationships, wood controls earth. One party is, therefore, clearly dominant, and, in this case, it is the Tiger who is in control. But the Dog does not mind. Their natural similarity softens the Tiger's touch and the Dog is content to let the Tiger be in charge.

In a match with the Horse, peace reigns:

Such an endearing couple, these two people have perfectly compatible temperaments. Theirs is a peaceful home where there is a noticeable absence of arguments and temper tantrums. They give in to each other most of the time, both being sensible and rational human beings. There is cooperation and communication between them, and even when the Horse occasionally grows restive, it does not affect the relationship, since the Dog is able to understand and is prepared to listen. Neither will attempt to dominate or compete with the

Tiger Years

1914
1926
1938
1950
1962
1974
1986
1998

Horse Years

1918
1930
1942
1954
1966
1978
1990
2002

other, and their natural affinity makes them trust each other implicitly. At work, the Horse will be the more aggressive, but the Dog is happy to let the Horse take the lead. In love, the two will be devoted to each other, being neither possessive nor interfering.

The Dog's natural element is earth, while the Horse's element is fire. In the cycle of element relationships, fire produces earth. One party is, therefore, clearly supportive of the other, and, in this case, it is the Horse who supports and provides for the Dog. Their instinctive sensitivity to each other, however, makes the restless and headstrong Horse more than happy to give generously of his or her time and understanding, while the Dog sits back and enjoys the Horse's loving attention!

103

Enhancing the love life of Boar people

**Boar
Years**
1 9 2 3
1 9 3 5
1 9 4 7
1 9 5 9
1 9 7 1
1 9 8 3
1 9 9 5
2 0 0 7

The Boar is the twelfth sign of the Chinese Zodiac. Its intrinsic element is water. The "hour" of the Boar is said to be between 9.00 and 11.00 p.m. Anyone who is born between those hours is said to be born in the hour of the Boar.

The compass direction of the Boar is between 307.5 and 337.5 degrees, so occupying 30 degrees. This falls in the direction of north-north-west, and is shown on the compass above, marked with the Boar.

This sector is said to be the part of the house that is most lucky for any of its inhabitants who were born in the years of the Boar, some of which are listed above. These years have not been adjusted to take account of the Lunar New Year. So, if you were born in any of the above years during January, you probably do not belong to the Boar year, but to the year prior to it, which is that of the Dog. Similarly, you could still be a Boar if you were born in the January of the following year. To check your date of birth against the lunar calendar, please refer to the 100-year lunar calendar at the front of this book.

To energize good love luck in your personal earthly branch sector, there are several symbolic things you can do:

Place images of the Boar in the sector of your house that falls between the degrees indicated above. To enhance this area's intrinsic energy, display Boar images next to water. This enhances the water element of this animal sign.

You can activate the sector with water features like aquariums and ponds, since water is the intrinsic element of your animal sign. However, it will be bad luck for you if a toilet or kitchen is placed there (i.e., the west-north-west), as this would seriously afflict your sector.

Boar year people also benefit from sectors that correspond to Sheep and Rabbit animal years. The direction of the Sheep is south-south-west, and the direction of the Rabbit is east.

The sensitive lady Boar and the decorous male Boar 104

Rabbit Years
1915
1927
1939
1951
1963
1975
1987
1999

Sheep Years
1919
1931
1943
1955
1967
1979
1991
2003

With the Rabbit it's a case of opposites attracting:

The Boar is loud and somewhat aggressive, while the Rabbit is quiet and subtle – a clear case of opposites attracting. The Boar has a tendency to use power and strength to get his/her way, while the Rabbit prefers to use his/her guile and intelligence to think carefully through problems, silently working in an unassertive fashion. Yet, the two appear to think alike, and to want the same things in life. Where they differ is the way they go about achieving their goals. When the two come together, it is like a blending of two complementary halves. There is a natural attraction between them from the start, and, when they discover each other's talents, the two get along like a house on fire. They also make a great team. While the Rabbit is happy to be manipulative from behind the scenes, the Boar enjoys being in the spotlight. Each brings out the best in the other.

The Boar's natural element is water while the Rabbit's is wood. In the cycle of element relationships, water produces wood. One party clearly provides the sustenance and support here, and it is the Boar, who is therefore deemed to be excellent good fortune for the Rabbit! This augurs very well for the alliance between the two of them.

The Sheep and the Boar make a genuinely happy pair:

The natural affinity of the Sheep and the Boar is reflected in their obvious concern for and patience with each other. The sensitive Sheep finds sustenance, comfort and love from the Boar, whose broad shoulders willingly enfold the Sheep in a warm cocoon of love. Nor is the Sheep merely a love object; indeed, the two find pleasure in working and planning their life together.

The earthy Boar admires the gentle and classy disposition of the Sheep. These two both have healthy appetites, and they are equally generous towards one another. In love, they enjoy life's simple pleasures, with neither one going off at a tangent or succumbing to outside distractions. Loyalty features very prominently in this relationship, and it is, therefore, one of the most compatible of the pairings in Chinese astrology.

The Sheep's natural element is earth, while the Boar's is water. In the cycle of element relationships, earth controls water. One party is clearly in control, and, in this case, it is the Sheep. Their instinctive sympathy smooths the interactions between them, and the more aggressive Boar gives in easily to the subtle and understated Sheep.

The Sheep obviously dominates this relationship, and it is not surprising as the Boar is neither as clever nor as worldly wise as the Sheep. Indeed, in this union, the Sheep will generally steer the Boar out of dangerous waters, and the latter will be happy to accept it with a smile and good grace!

105 Beware the astrological arrows of antagonism

In the Chinese Zodiac wheel, arrows of antagonism are said to be created between animal signs that are placed directly opposite each other. These indicate generalized readings of incompatibility between the horoscope signs affected.

Based on this belief, there are six sets of major incompatibilities between the twelve animal signs. On the zodiac wheel, reproduced here, these animals are those that "confront" each other. All individuals, depending on the animal signs under which they are born, will tend to reveal specific types of behavior, especially with respect to the way they respond and react to others. This inner nature, which is unconscious, is often the cause of deep-seated conflict between incompatible partners. It is for this reason that many Chinese parents frown on matches between their children and anyone who is six years younger or older, since they know that serious difficulties between them will surface should they marry. Nevertheless, the reader should understand that characteristics of individuals often get magnified, or diminished by element influences and ascendant hours of birth. In addition, please note that incompatibilities between clashing animal signs show up and become evident only within close relationships as in a marriage or a close business partnership. Incompatibilities often do not prevent them from becoming good friends. This is because good friends do not have to live or work together. In a love match, however, these incompatibilities should never be ignored or brushed aside. Steps should always be taken to reduce any problems that arise out of the incompatibility that is shown.

Chinese zodiac wheel

- The Rat (water) clashes with the Horse (fire)
- The Ox (earth) clashes with the Sheep (earth)
- The Tiger (wood) clashes with the Monkey (metal)
- The Dragon (earth) clashes with the Dog (earth)
- The Rooster (metal) clashes with the Rabbit (wood)
- The Snake (fire) clashes with the Boar (water)

Above: Knowing about the hidden astrological arrows of antagonism should alert you to potentially difficult relationships.

A Rat and a Horse can create bad vibes

This is one of the worst matches of the Chinese Zodiac. It represents a clash of strong wills. There is a complete absence of communication between these two. Unless their ascendant hours and elements are compatible, this pairing is best split apart before it becomes established. The free-spirited attitude of the Horse simply clashes too badly with the snobbish tendencies of the insecure Rat. Also, the Horse lacks the drive and social-climbing ambitions which galvanize the Rat. The Horse's impulsive nature will annoy the Rat after their initial attraction fades and what was considered attractive becomes a bone of contention. Their attitude towards each other is combative, and their elements clash badly – water with fire. Since both are intrinsically yang neither is prepared to be yielding.

To overcome and reduce the

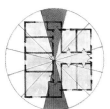

Rat's N location

Horse's S location

negative effect of this clashing incompatibility between a Rat and Horse, it is first important to understand the influence of the five elements upon their relationship.

The natural element of someone born during a Rat year is water, while that of the Horse is fire. In the cycle of the five elements, water controls fire. The Rat will, therefore, tend to dominate the Horse. But because the Horse is

free-spirited and independent, this attempt to control him/her will meet with fierce resistance and arguments.

To overcome this mismatch of temperaments, find sectors in the home which correspond to them, and then enhance each one with a harmonious element. The Rat's sector is in the north, while the Horse's is in the south. Place metal (a wind chime) in the Rat sector, and a plant in the Horse sector. Strengthening the luck of both parties should go a long way to appeasing them.

As an extra measure, the Rat person should enhance his/her luck by incorporating white colours into his/her wardrobe, or by wearing feng shui jewellery. The double-happiness ring * would be superb. The Horse person, on the other hand, will benefit by wearing red or green colours.

Rats of marriageable age are those born in 1960 (metal Rat: 39 years of age in 1999) or 1972 (water Rat: 27 years old in 1999).

Horses of marriagable age are those who were born in 1966 (fire Horse: 33 years of age in 1999) or 1978 (earth Horse: 21 years old in 1999).

The Ox and the Sheep – a clumsy pair

Petulance and exasperation characterize this relationship. The nature of the Ox and the Sheep are totally dissimilar. The Ox is a no-nonsense sort of person who has little time to waste on emotion, while the Sheep, although not head-strong or impulsive, nevertheless tends to be emotional. These two have different priorities, and their views about life and love diverge. Each perceives the other as doing things the wrong way, and going off in the wrong direction. So, while both are ambitious, and can be highly motivated, their characters do not allow them to see eye-to-eye, nor to appreciate the other. This is a pity because their complementary skills could well make them a great pair. Unfortunately, they are not sufficiently compatible to be able to take advantage of each other's attributes and strengths.

Usually, the Ox person likes to think things through sensibly and carefully,

Ox's NNE location

Sheep's SSW location

preferring his/her own counsel. The Sheep, on the other hand, likes consulting others and listening to other people's views. The fact that both the Sheep and the Ox can be dogmatic and stubborn does not help. Theirs will be more of an adversarial interaction.

The Sheep's natural element is earth, and so is that of the Ox. There is too much earth energy in this coupling, with the disadvantage that it is being channeled in different directions.

Too much stubbornness exists in this personality combination; their energies are not compatible. This truly is a difficult match with little potential, so it would be much better for both people to move on. However, should they decide to marry, or are already married, feng shui may help to reduce any friction and hostility.

Note that a marriage between a water Ox and an earth Sheep favours the Sheep, since the element of the year strengthens his/her spirit. Still, the Ox is not in any way handicapped by the elements. However, the match remains awkward.

The problem between these two is an excess of earth energy. It would help to exhaust this energy a little by hanging metal wind chimes in the home, particularly in the two corners which correspond to the Ox and Sheep.

Oxen of marriageable age are those who were born in 1961 (metal Ox: 38 years of age in 1999) or 1973 (water Ox: 26 years old in 1999).

Sheep of marriageable age are those who were born in 1967 (fire Sheep: 32 years old in 1999) or 1979 (earth Sheep: 20 in 1999).

108

The Tiger and the Monkey – more hate than love

Tigers of marriageable age are those who were born in 1962 (water Tiger: 37 years of age in 1999) or 1974 (wood Tiger: 25 years old in 1999).

Monkeys of marriageable age are those who were born in 1968 (earth Monkey: 31 in 1999) or 1980 (metal Monkey: 19 years old in 1999).

These two impetuous yang individuals are irresistibly drawn towards each other from the start. Theirs is an intimacy full of laughter and adventure, loaded with intensity and energy. There is also a great deal of passion between them, with dramatic break-ups and equally emotional reconciliations. However, it is an intense love-hate friendship, except there is increasingly more hate than love as it continues. They continually match wits and challenge each other – neither being prepared to give in to the other. They are both poor losers, and there is nothing graceful or diplomatic in their interchange. Both are highly individual, determined and impulsive. If their relationship works, it will be because they understand their own strong and extrovert natures. However, because they are naturally incompatible, it is

Tiger's NE location

Monkey's SW location

more likely that the couple will suffer a dramatic and hostile break-up. Their magnificent fights will exhaust them to the point of breakdown. A Tiger-Monkey partnership could end up being one long yelling match!

The Tiger's natural element is wood. The Monkey's is metal. Metal controls wood, so it will be the Monkey who dominates the relationship and takes

the lead – which is just as well. The Tiger's ferocity is no match for the Monkey's ingenuity, but this will also make Tigers fight back below the belt.

Partnerships between the wood Tiger and the earth Monkey are good because they are aided by the elements, which work in favour of this match. The Tiger benefits from the strength provided by the wood element, while the Monkey is energized by the earth element, which produces metal! This favourable element influence gives the alliance a chance of success, bringing resilience and strength to both parties.

Tiger-Monkey couples with other configurations can consider strengthening elements by placing bright lights in both the Tiger's direction (east-north-east) and the Monkey's direction (west-south-west). This should reduce their incompatibility.

109

The Rooster and Rabbit – a mediocre sex life

Roosters of marriageable age are those born in 1969 (earth Rooster: 30 years of age in 1999) or 1981 (metal Rooster: 18 years old in 1999).

Rabbits of marriageable age are those born in 1963 (water Rabbit: 26 years old in 1999) or 1975 (wood Rabbit: 24 years old in 1999).

This pair could not be further apart in terms of what each consider to be proper behaviour. The Rooster finds the Rabbit's righteous morality insufferable and the Rabbit regards the Rooster's arrogance and pretensions annoying. The Rabbit is low-profile and understated, while the Rooster is smug and conceited, carrying a know-it-all attitude in a manner that thoroughly grates on the Rabbit's nerves.

In the zodiac, these two are supposedly natural enemies. They suffer the negative effects of each other's poison arrows, thereby bringing out the worst in one another. The Rabbit's traditional reserve turns into disdainful indifference while the Rooster's boastful nature is carried to such extremes as to become distasteful. They are truly bad for one another. As long as they don't have to live with each

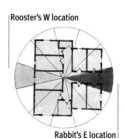

Rooster's W location

Rabbit's E location

other, or see and interact with each other on a daily basis, they could perhaps be good friends ... but once married, the Rabbit will regard the Rooster as nothing but a pompous show-off while the Rooster will sniff haughtily at and reject the Rabbit's virtuous holier than thou attitude.

Besides, sex between the Rooster and the Rabbit is at best mediocre!

The influence of the elements

The Rooster's natural element is metal. The Rabbit's natural element is wood. In the cycle of elements, metal controls wood. This indicates that it is the Rooster who will control and dominate the Rabbit, or at least attempt to do so. But whether the Rabbit is prepared to accept the Rooster's leadership is something else again! Based on the zodiac readings this is quite unlikely, and being a yin animal, the Rooster will be unable to really achieve much in terms of domination over the similarly yin Rabbit. Marriage between the Rooster and the Rabbit can be made a lot better if the natural chi of each animal's element is suitably strengthened. The Rooster should always wear gold jewellery while the Rabbit will benefit by wearing a lot of green. Both men and women would benefit from wearing jade.

The Dragon and the Dog bark all night long

These two are naturally incompatible! It is improbable they will even find each other attractive. The spirited and impulsive Dragon has no time for the cynically inclined Dog personality. They cannot hold a conversation without one of them coming near to losing his/her cool. It is better that such a match does not become permanent. In the zodiac, their signs are placed directly in the path of each other's arrow of antagonism; and they are regarded as intrinsic enemies. The Dog will sniff with disdain at the Dragon's ideas and opinions, while the Dragon finds the Dog hostile, unsupportive and a wet blanket! This match is a serious example of clashing personalities. Not only is there little communication between them, there will be much exhaling in exasperation on the part of the Dragon, and a great deal of shrill barking from the Dog! The two

avoiding each other altogether is the best way to deal with the continious friction between them; otherwise both will get hurt.

Both the Dog and the Dragon are earth signs, and both are yang. This preponderance of earth and yang energy will accentuate the hostility between them, and bring out all their naturally aggressive instincts. Unless the hour ascendants cool down their

Dog's WNW location

Dragon's ESE location

tempers, it is best that they part!

Marriage between the fire Dragon and the metal Dog will be unhappy. If the Dog is the male (as is likely, as he's older), this will be a case of a hen-pecked husband, and an strong wife.

Partnerships between a wood Dragon and a metal Dog are inauspicious for both! The Dragon is weakened, and the Dog exhausted, by their interaction. This union is likely to end in separation or divorce, which will cause less suffering.

My advice is for Dragons and Dogs not to get together. If you are already are, the best way to reduce friction between you is to place a big urn filled with water in your respective compass sectors. The water can also be placed near your home's entrance. The idea is to contain your anger and unhappiness.

Dragons of marriageable age are those who were born in 1964 (wood Dragon: 35 years of age in 1999) or 1976 (fire Dragon: 23 years old in 1999).

Dogs of marriageable age are those born in 1970 (metal Dog: 29 in 1999) or 1982 (water Dog: 17 years old in 1999).

The Snake and the Boar – a sad mismatch

There is absolutely no compatibility between these two – making it one of the worst personality combinations of the zodiac. The Snake and the Boar never see eye-to-eye, and disagree on everything. Anything done by one for the other is not appreciated, and is a waste of time, effort, and money! So, all the good intentions in the world cannot save this partnership from degenerating into unhappiness. Misunderstanding of motives and intentions rule the day, and, in the end, both sides will give up trying altogether. Besides, the two are different in so many other ways. Communication between them will simply be completely absent. Ordinarily, the Boar is obliging, considerate and kind, but all of this will come across as naive, weak and dumb to the haughty Snake! The same is true of the Snake's good intentions. His/her propensity towards deep thought and

planning will be interpreted as pretension and indecisiveness by the Boar. Both will find fault with the other continually, and neither can win.

This is further borne out by the natural antipathy of their elements. The Snake's intrinsic element is fire. The Boar's is water. In the element cycle water controls fire. So the Boar will want to control and dominate. Both signs are

Boar's NW location

Snake's SE location

yin, and yielding should come easily to them, but, in this case, yin merely hides the anger of yang.

An analysis of the marriage prospects of the fire Snake and the metal Boar can be misleading. Both appear to have elements that add sparkle and energy to their intrinsic natures. This is not necessarily a good thing, however, because, although these elements bring good luck to the pair, they do not bring happiness. The Snake will revert to his/her true self, and the Boar will be unable to understand what has gone wrong. Therefore, these animals should avoid each other. If already together, the way to reduce friction is to strengthen the elements of the sectors representing them. The Snake should benefit from plants in the south (south-south-east, actually), while the Boar will benefit from a bright light in the north-north-west.

Snakes of marriageable age are those who were born in 1965 (wood Snake: 34 years of age in 1999) or 1977 (fire Snake: 22 years old in 1999).

Boars of marriageable age are those who were born in 1971 (metal Boar: 28 years old in 1999) or 1959 (earth Boar: 40 in 1999).

112

Boost marriage happiness by choosing good dates

Apart from the six commonly accepted poor pairings just mentioned, which are contained in conventional astrological texts, there are also a great many other partnerships that could end in unhappiness due to other reasons. Incompatibility can manifest as a result of disharmony of elements contained in the parties' Four Pillars Chart (although Three Pillars is often sufficient to reveal instances of chronic incompatibility). The Three Pillars I usually refer to are the month, year and hour of birth. I leave out the day of birth simply because its influence on compatibility readings is marginal and it takes too much effort to work out.

Incompatibilities, for instance, can, and often are, overcome when extra care is taken to ensure that a marriage is held on an auspicious day. The date of the wedding dinner and ceremony should be properly worked out, based on the Lo Shu numbers of different auspicious dates as well as the horoscope charts of the couple. This calculation of auspicious dates is extremely important and it represents an integral part of advanced feng shui calculations. (I am working on a book that shows how all of the various auspicious dates may be calculated, but this will not be available until the year 2001.) Usually, most Chinese refer to the Almanac for calculating good dates, but this is not reliable unless you refer to the authentic Chinese Almanac.

My recommendation for those who do not know how to calculate auspicious days is to choose dates that correspond to the first day of the new moon. It is not always the best date available, but it is invariably better than getting married on an inauspicious day, as it symbolizes a new beginning. The night of the full moon is also a good time, since it honours the God of Marriage, who is believed to live on the moon. The moon is also excellent yin energy.

When people marry on an auspicious day – i.e., a day when all the elements work harmoniously – any incompatibility between them is instantly diminished. Sometimes the potency of the good day is so strong, it brings great fortune to the couple as well.

Left: Getting married on a date close to a new moon will help to diminish any incompatibility between couples.

Gift offerings to enhance marriage luck

The exchange of offerings is often extremely auspicious and helpful in mitigating some of the hurdles caused by incompatible horoscope readings. Generally, the source of incompatibility between couples is disharmony in the five elements in their respective birth charts. For instance, if the horoscope of the bride lacks the element, fire, and that of the bridegroom has an excess of water, then, because water controls fire, the marriage will cause the bride to lack energy. The husband will make things worse with his excess of water.

A gift that suggests the fire element should be given to the bride by the groom at the time of their marriage to symbolize that the yang energy of fire is being embellished just for her benefit. The gift would make things more harmonious between them. It would be wonderful, then, if the bridegroom gave his wife a pair of red shoes, a red evening dress, ruby earrings, cheek blusher, a red bedspread and a pair of bright red lanterns. All of these manifest the fire element, and are suitable as gifts when there is a lack of fire in a woman's horoscope. The bride can undertake the same analysis when selecting gifts for her husband.

Suggestions for the other four elements are:

To compensate for a lack of water, give blue outfits, sapphires, aquamarines, goldfish and blue lamps.
To compensate for a lack of earth, give all kinds of semi-precious gemstones and crystals.
To compensate for a lack of wood, give silk flowers, paintings of auspicious flowers and healthy, leafy plants.
To compensate for a lack of metal, give plenty of gold.

Gifts of this kind are not the traditional good fortune ones given as part of the marriage ritual. They are modern-day adaptations based on the theory and method of wu xing or "five element compensation".

According to the *Book of Rites*, this giving ritual is conducted in order to express mutual wishes for fidelity, protection and successful procreation. An auspicious number of gifts is eight. The bridegroom should send eight gifts to his bride, among which should be:

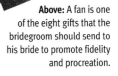

Above: A fan is one of the eight gifts that the bridegroom should send to his bride to promote fidelity and procreation.

- a piece of gold jewellery for her hair, as this will be auspicious
- a gilt mirror to protect her from bad chi and evil spirits
- a box of chocolates or sweetmeats to wish her a sweet life
- a length of red brocade or silk for her material happiness
- a gift of money (coins and notes) for her brothers and parents
- a painting portraying a child and fish to signify successful childbirth
- a bunch of peonies (can be made of silk) for marital happiness
- a sandalwood fan to signify that she will have his protection all her life

Wear red at your wedding to enhance yang energy

In Chinese weddings, the bride is always elaborately dressed in a red ceremonial wedding dress. This dress is customarily decorated with beads, crystals and sometimes even precious stones, depending on the wealth of her family. It is believed that when her wedding apparel is encrusted with jewels, she will bring great good fortune to the marriage. In addition, this outfit will have elaborate embroidery featuring all the auspicious symbols that signify a happy, fruitful match. These symbols include the Dragon-Phoenix pair, peonies and the double-happiness sign.

However, brides should never have their wedding dresses made until they have definite marriage plans. An old wives' tale suggests that to buy a wedding dress, or even a marriage bed, prematurely causes bad luck that negates one's chances of getting married.

So do not buy an antique wedding bed for your unmarried daughters!

I always recommend that Chinese brides marry in red, especially for the celebration feast. They should definitely never wear black, as this is much too yin for what should be a yang occasion. It could also cause a senior relative (like a father or an uncle) who is attending the celebrations to succumb to serious illness that could prove fatal. The Chinese refer to this as being seriously affected by the yin energy emanated.

Black is not good for weddings

Remember that the bride must not wear black at her own wedding. I once attended an elaborate wedding dinner where the bride actually wore a stunning black evening dress as one of her many changes of outfits. I recall there was an audible gasp when she made an appearance, for everyone attending the wedding was familiar with this particular taboo. I felt sad that no one in her family had advised her. Sadly six months later, her father died of a heart attack!

Guests also should not wear black to a wedding, as this is deemed to be insensitive. If they wear red, they will heighten yang energy. Yellows and other bright colours will also add yang energy to the occasion.

Left: Although, traditionally, western brides wear a white dress at weddings, it is a good idea to wear something red or pink as a going away outfit. Alternatively, make sure that red is included in some way in your ceremony, such as having a red car or red flowers.

Enhancing the eight sectors of the marital home

An excellent feng shui ritual that enhances chi and brings harmony, many descendants and a long, happy marriage should precede a couple moving into a home. Choose a good day when the sun is shining brightly, and undertake this ceremony well before 12 noon. It will reduce any stress or tension between the couple caused by horoscope incompatibility, and dissolve bad luck from the eight corners of the home.

Finding the right sector

In the sector that represents the area where the main door is located, do this ritual three times in order to ensure that elemental energies are suitably enhanced. Start at the main front door and move in a clockwise direction, from corner to corner. If the main door is positioned in the east, start in the east, and then move to the south-east, south, and so forth. And if the main door is located in the north, start at the north and then move to the north-east. You must mark the eight outside sectors of the home on a layout plan in order to do this ritual efficiently.

For the north: Fill a jug with water, mix some saffron in the water and, once it has turned yellow, sprinkle it all over the part of the home that falls within the north sector of the home. Do this on each floor.

For the north-east and south-west: Obtain some river or sea sand and fill a pail with it.

Above: If you need to enhance the north-east and south-west sectors of your home, mix the ash from incense sticks with sand and sprinkle it in these areas.

Light three incense sticks and mix the ash from them. Then throw the sand over the north-east and south-west sectors. This energizes good earth energy in these two earth areas. Do this both upstairs and downstairs. Keep the soil there for a day before sweeping and cleaning it away.

For the east and south-east: Pluck seven types of auspicious flowers. They can be in any colours. Ideally, make them chrysanthemums, peonies, lilies, orchids, plum and lotus blossoms, and bulb flowers. If this is not possible, try to include flowers from each of the four seasons to symbolize year-round harmony and auspicious luck. Sprinkle flower petals in these two wood sectors to symbolize the flowering of wealth, prosperity and good health luck. Some Taoist masters also advise sprinkling seeds to ensure that good descendants come from the marriage.

For the south: Light three red candles in this sector to energize yang energy.

For the west and north-west: Place three gold pieces or silver ornaments on a platter. Carry it around the rooms comprising these sectors so that the symbolism of metal will enhance the chi there.

These rituals are said to enhance all the sectors of the home, and may be repeated each year, preferably any day between the first and the fifteenth day of the Lunar New Year.

116

How to reduce bad luck from the ten directions

This ritual is said to ward off bad luck from the ten directions and is recommended for use before embarking on a long journey. My Tibetan Buddhist master who translated it from an old text gave this excellent technique to me. When I shared it with feng shui master Yap Cheng Hai, he immediately recognized it and revealed that it was also excellent for "cleansing" – particularly newlyweds.

The ten directions referred to are the eight main directions of the compass. The ninth direction is that which is above, and the tenth is what is from below. To overcome bad luck from all of the ten directions that surround your home, hold a curved metal knife high above your head, then swing it from left to right and from right to left – three times each way.

The curved knife need not be very large. The largest I have found is about 20cm (8in)

long. I have seen curved knives in the markets of Thamel in Kathmandu, Nepal, but I am told they can also be found in India and China. Alternatively, use any metal cutting instrument.

Master Yap also revealed that, in addition to using the curved knife, you can make a mixture of rice and salt and sprinkle it in all sectors of a new home – inside and outside, just before moving into it. A preparation of sea salt and rice is especially useful since the salt carries the powerful cleansing energy of the oceans. Walk from room to room, sprinkling this mixture on the floor as you move in a clockwise direction in each room. While doing this visualize that you are cleansing the chi of your home with the salt, while you are offering the rice to appease any land spirits which may be present. Think "let us live happily ever together". Leave for a night and day after doing the ritual before sweeping up.

117

Double-happiness symbol brings marital luck

It stands to reason that happiness chi is most efficiently created by the word itself doubled. Therefore, the most powerful and widely recognized symbol of marital happiness is the double-happiness sign, shown here on the left.

The symbol surpasses even the Dragon-Phoenix symbol on wedding cards, invitations and home decorations. Carved onto marital beds, chairs and other bedroom furniture, it ensures continued good fortune for a couple. In the past, this symbol was almost always specially painted or stamped upon wedding gifts given to newlyweds by elders and relatives.

Displaying double-happiness calligraphy in the home can help ensure that a marriage is happy. It is said to be effective for two people with incompatible astrological charts. This is based on the belief that auspicious calligraphy always manifests in the words written. So often auspicious Chinese characters are written and displayed prominently in old Chinese mansions.

Hang the double-happiness sign in the bedroom – especially on the wall that represents your personalized marriage direction based on the Eight Mansions or KUA formula. This successfully creates excellent marriage happiness chi.

Good fortune symbols for couples

There are three important happy occasions in any person's life which, according to feng shui, should be surrounded with good fortune symbols.

The three occasions are:
1) The first month birthday celebration of the first-born son.
2) Wedding day ceremonies, especially the journey of the bride to the bride-groom's house for the wedding ceremony.
3) Birthday celebrations of the family patriarch when his is 69, 79 and 89.

It is thought to be excellent feng shui for the bride to go to her wedding in a carriage or car that contains all of the good fortune symbols. First of all, the car should be red. In China in the past, the groom's party always came to collect the bride from her parents' home in a red sedan chair that would be elaborately decorated with auspicious symbols like the double-happiness sign or the Dragon-Phoenix image. Today, of course, the sedan chair is out of date, but its red colour continues to have significance. If you cannot find a red car, acceptable alternative colours are those that signify happy, auspicious yang energy. Thus, maroon, yellow and white would all be acceptable. Do not get married in yin colours or in a yin-coloured car.

Above: An old Chinese tradition at wedding receptions was to greet the arrival of the bridal pair with red firecrackers.

It is an excellent idea to tie the endless knot, which symbolizes undying love between the couple, to the front of the car. When the couple arrives at the place where the wedding dinner or party is to be held, it is always a good idea for them to be greeted by a loud sound. In the old days, firecrackers would be set off to herald the start of the celebration. A modern adaptation for this would be a live band striking up a wedding march to represent clashing yang energy.

The carriage used by the couple on the wedding day signifies a glorious start to a new beginning. It is important that nothing happens to the carriage. If a car stops, stalls, or meets with an accident, it is not a good omen and signifies obstacles. If something like this happens, or for any reason the car breaks down, then someone with the bridal couple should swing a curved knife through the air three times – right to left and left to right. This is believed to overcome any bad chi that may be coming and dissolve it.

Yin and Yang Colours

Yin colours
All shades of:
Blue
Black
Brown

Yang colours
Red
Maroon
Yellow
White

(The colour purple may be yin or yang depending on the circumstances.)

119 Boost a crystal heart with moon energy for love

Because the heart shape is so widely recognized as a universal symbol of love, and because earth energy in feng shui is so strongly associated with marriage and auspicious family luck, crystal hearts are wonderful for attracting marriage luck. It is, therefore, a very good idea to look for decorative heart symbols that are made of quartz crystals or any other kind of semi-precious stones, which signify strong earth energy. I like rose quartz and Taiwan red coral, since these suggest this.

It is not a good idea to have hearts that are made of blue or green-coloured stones. A blue heart always suggests a short-lived romance. Hearts should also not be made of tiger's-eye, malachite or lapis lazuli. You really should use crystals if you plan to use stone hearts to activate your marriage luck.

To make your crystal heart a powerful energizer, allow it to soak up the moon's energy.

Choose a night when the moon is full and the sky is clear. Place the crystal heart in a high place in the garden or on your terrace and allow it to be bathed in the magical glow of the moonlight. Remember that the god of marriage is said to reside in the moon. If possible, let your crystal heart absorb three nights' worth of moon energy.

Placing crystal in your nien yen area

Then place this crystal in the nien yen part of your bedroom. The nien yen sector is your marriage and family area, and its location is based upon your date of birth and gender (see Tip 68 on the KUA and Eight Mansions formula). If you are already sleeping with your head pointed in your nien yen direction, place the crystal heart under your pillow.

Once you have put these feng shui energizers in place, forget about them and let them do their work. Do not be too anxious to meet someone as negative chi creates blockages and possible obstacles. So, relax and stay cool.

Left: A pink or red crystal heart made from rose quartz or red coral, when energized by the moon, can help you find a partner when you place it in your nien yen area in your bedroom.

The lute signifies perfect union

The sounds produced by the Chinese stringed instrument referred to as the lute are said to be so harmonious that they signify a state of perfect union between two people. It has, therefore, long been regarded as an emblem of matrimonial happiness.

Lutes go far back in history to the time of Fu Hsi, the legendary emperor who wrote the *I Ching*. Lutes produce hauntingly beautiful music. The nearest thing to them are probably western violins.

Beautiful music

The sound of the lute is believed to express not merely the sexual bliss of matrimony but, more importantly, to exemplify friendship between patriarch and matriarch. Both purity and moderation are invoked by the lute's sweet sound, so the instrument came to symbolize harmony and happiness in family life. It was also said to be a reminder of one of the amiable singing of pine trees, and to produce thoughts of fidelity.

Traditional ancient lutes are reputed to have been made of wood from the Phoenix tree. Ritual soaking of the wood often accompanied the production of lutes.

Originally the lute had five strings that emitted five notes; these corresponded to the five elements – wood, fire, earth, metal and water. Later, seven strings, and so the two additional elements of wind and air, were added.

The lute is credited as having eight attributes, namely: happiness, elegance, sweetness, subtlety, nostalgia, softness, resonance and strength. These are qualities that describe matrimonial and family happiness. If you hang a painting that shows a woman playing this

Above: A violin, like the traditional lute, has eight attributes linked to marital happiness. So display a painting of a woman playing one to encourage marital happiness.

musical instrument, it will be most beneficial.

In recent times, the flute also has come to be regarded as similarly auspicious for marital harmony. So, paintings of beautiful female Chinese flute players dressed in traditional silks and brocades have become extremely popular. They are also extremely good feng shui! In this context, the magnificent paintings of Chen Yi Fei are especially suitable. Not many people can afford Chen's paintings, but there are many Chinese oil painters who have taken their cue from Chen and started painting musical instruments being played by beautiful women. Displaying paintings like these in your living room is most auspicious.

121 Red lanterns attract fertility

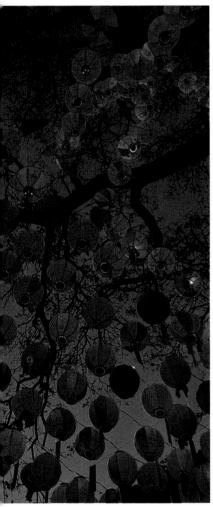

Above: Red and yellow lanterns are considered by the Chinese to be strong fertility symbols and were often placed in the marital bedroom.

Marriage luck in feng shui always goes hand-in-hand with descendants' luck. The Chinese believe that there can be no good fortune without descendants. And marriage luck is deemed to be missing when this is not accompanied by the ability to have children. Traditional Chinese people considered the ability to have children so important that men were encouraged to have second wives if the principal wife failed to bear children. So, feng shui also addresses this aspect of marital happiness.

In symbolic feng shui, there are many different symbols of fertility, but probably the most popular and commonly used symbol is the red lantern. Chinese literature is filled with poetry that describes the way lanterns cast auspicious light onto marital beds, enhancing the sleeping area and bringing occasions of great joy to families. Lanterns on which auspicious characters or beautiful symbols are painted have always been regarded as emblems of fertility. Therefore, to enhance the speedy conception of a child, lamps were often strategically placed near the bridal bed.

Sometimes, two red lanterns were hung – one on each side of the bridal bed – for the bride and groom. These lamps were lit together and, if they burned at the same rate, going out at the same time, it was regarded as an auspicious sign as it indicated a long and happy marriage. Such lamps would often have the auspicious double-happiness word printed on them, and these came in various designs. They were believed to attract yang chi, which often caused conception and led to the birth of a son. When the wife became pregnant, the lamp continued to be lit each night.

Auspicious lanterns

Lanterns were generally considered to be such amazingly auspicious symbols that a special day was set aside each year to celebrate a lantern festival. This was the fifteenth day of the first Chinese month, which also coincides with the last day of the Lunar New Year celebrations.

A second lantern festival was held on the seventh day of the seventh moon, when the seven beautiful sisters of Heaven were said to descend to earth. My mother used to tell me that, on this night, the seven sisters would pass by homes that displayed lanterns and drop a little of their magical moon powder onto them, which would mingle with the ash from special fragrant joss sticks burned on altars for the occasion. This magical moon powder was said to enhance the beauty of unmarried maidens, and assist them to attract handsome husbands! To attract the seven heavenly sisters into the home, lanterns, similar to those pictured here, can be hung beside the entrance door.

How to create auspicious descendants' luck

Above: For centuries, the Chinese believed it was good fortune to have many sons, but today a healthy child of either sex is welcomed.

There is a very famous painting that shows 100 children playing in a garden. All the children drawn are boys, and this painting is believed to be most auspicious as a gift to a pregnant woman, as it indicates many sons!

In many Chinese and Asian cultures, families usually considered sons to represent great good fortune, while daughters were rather unwelcome. This Chinese desire for sons was, for many centuries, extremely persistent. Even as recently as the twentieth century, parents in China, weighed down by the one-child rule, often abandoned baby girls so that they could try again for a male child. Happily, this attitude is completely absent among modern and overseas Chinese. Nevertheless, traditional attitudes like this do not die easily.

It is said that many masterpieces with this subject – begetting sons – used to hang in the bedchamber of the Chinese Emperor. They symbolized the wish that the "son of heaven" would produce many male heirs, since this was regarded as the surest way of perpetuating the dynastic system. According to the *Book of Odes*, an old Chinese classic of customs and folklore,

a woman will bear a son if she dreams of black, brown or white bears while she is pregnant. If she dreams of snakes, she will have a daughter.

Usually, the best gifts for a pregnant woman were considered to be auspicious paintings with symbolic meanings. One showing a boy mounted on a unicorn, or holding a lotus, signified the wish for sons. A painting of twelve children with peaches and pomegranates means, "May you have a long life and plenty of children"! A painting of an old man with a child was thought to be auspicious, as it meant wishing the pregnant woman a particularly clever son. The old man here is supposed to represent the Taoist sage Lao Tze.

Having clever sons

The aspiration of giving birth to a clever son capable of performing brilliantly at the imperial exams was a prime aspiration of Chinese parents for over 2,000 years. This was because the examinations were the best way of attaining success and high rank in the Emperor's court, a success that would benefit the entire family. It is not so different in today's world! Education is still key to great success.

So, if you want to present a particularly apt gift with this auspicious meaning, I suggest you give a painting that depicts a Dragon – better yet, a Dragon carp. This means a carp with the body of a fish, but the head of a Dragon. It implies the successful crossing of the "Dragon gate" – in legend, the carp swimming against the current and leaping over the gate to be transformed into a Dragon. Also, it symbolizes the successful completion of exams and joining of the august ranks of officials.

123

How celebrating births brings good luck

dress. I considered the customary auspicious red to be excessively yang for her, because she already had too much fire in her birth chart!

But I did send eggs dyed red to my parents and in-laws, and celebrated her first-month birthday with an elaborate, expensive dinner. This kind of celebration is said to bring good fortune to a family, since it announces a hei see, which attracts good chi into the home. It is, therefore, better to hold the celebration dinner at home, because lots of people coming to the home brings yang energy into it.

Also, gifts of gold for the baby – bangles, bracelets and little gold coins – are symbolically very auspicious. When you are invited to a baby's month-old celebration dinner, do offer a small gift of gold to the child. This is very meaningful from a feng shui point of view!

One negative result of horoscope incompatibility was believed to be a lack of descendants' luck. Since the birth of a son (and heir) was always regarded as being an extremely happy occasion, it is considered to be extremely good feng shui to celebrate and commemorate the occasion.

Sons were particularly welcome in the rich and powerful families of old China. Sons would carry on the family name. Girls were regarded as unimportant, since they were expected to eventually marry and leave the family. So, the birth of sons was always a greater cause for celebration than the birth of daughters.

Today, of course, we celebrate both impartially. We therefore observe all the good fortune rituals equally for both sons and daughters.

I did, when my daughter Jennifer was born, since she was just as precious to me as a son. When she was born, I gave her a long pink

Above: In China gold coins are symbolically auspicious to give to a newborn baby.

Left: Sending reddyed eggs to relatives is said to create some good luck for a new child.

Don't send red roses with thorns

I know how romantic it must seem to send or receive long-stemmed red roses. Red roses have always symbolized a universal expression of romantic love, and, indeed, on Valentine's Day, there is such a premium on dark red roses that people often have to order bouquets of them well before February 14th.

However, according to feng shui, dark red flowers usually carry a negative connotation, and are believed to be especially harmful when sent as a get-well offering to someone who is lying ill in hospital. For lovers, dark red flowers also have a negative connotation – they usually indicate that the relationship will soon end.

Red roses with thorns actually send out a double message, which has a negative impact upon love relationships. When thorns are not removed from stems, the roses' negative impact is doubled; it is very likely that the relationship between sender and receiver will end. Indeed, I have seen some pretty strong friendships broken by this. I even know of marriages that have succumbed to this astonishingly strong negative energy.

In some eastern traditions, the colour red signifies death when brought close to someone convalescing from an illness. I am told that, in some hospitals, nurses familiar with some of these esoteric beliefs will never bring bouquets that contain red flowers into the private rooms and wards of patients.

It is important to note that it is not roses which bring bad luck. Indeed, yellow roses (with thorns taken off) are deemed to be extremely auspicious, as are yellow lilies and yellow daffodils, and all other yellow flowers. It is the colour red and thorns which together

are considered negative. To maximize the feng shui of love when you send flowers to loved ones, therefore, select yellow ones. These signify bright yang energy as well as the wonderful subdued energy of the earth. Bouquets for lovers should always contain fresh young leaves that indicate growth. This signifies the start of new beginnings and also indicates the growth chi of the wood element, and is, therefore, most auspicious for budding romances, or for bringing fresh vigour into a marriage that has become stale and stagnant.

Other lucky colours for flowers that add to, rather than detract from, relationships are pinks and lilac. These are fine when displayed in homes, since they add yin balance to yang bouquets.

Finally, give fresh flowers, rather than artificial flowers, and do not offer dried flowers. The connotation of dried flowers is death.

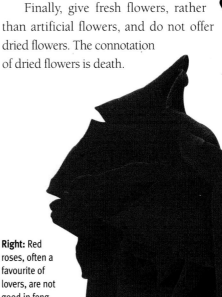

Right: Red roses, often a favourite of lovers, are not good in feng shui. Yellow ones, however, with thorns removed will bring good luck.

125 A traditional tea ceremony for good marriage luck

The Chinese and the English share a similar passion for drinking tea. To the Chinese, however, tea drinking is steeped in many cultural traditions, and is associated with many auspicious effects. Perhaps the most significant tea drinking ritual is that associated with the marriage ceremony. Newly married couples, dressed in their wedding clothes, participate in this ritual, which honours and invokes blessings from their elders. According to Chinese cultural tradition, blessings from the older generation carry great potency.

So, the newly married bride and groom, resplendent in their wedding finery, are supposed to kneel in front of their respective parents and to offer each of them a small cup of the finest tea. Their parents should accept the tea, signifying their approval of the match. They then bless the couple before offering them a red packet filled with money, jewellery and

Below: Drinking tea with their parents at a couple's marriage, before being blessed and given money is a Chinese tradition still practised today.

other goodies. According to custom, the more refined the tea, the larger the offering is considered to be. Also, the higher the monetary value of the red packet, the more auspicious it is for the start of the couple's married life.

Money offerings

In old China, a bride's parents often presented gold to their departing daughter after the performance of the tea ceremony. This was deemed to be an auspicious offering.

In modern times, this has been replaced with a red packet of cash. Indeed, in keeping with this, wealthy parents have been known to give the deeds of a property as well as stock certificates to their newly married sons and daughters. Paper wealth now seems to replace gold!

Out of respect, tea must also be offered to every member of the family who is one generation older than the couple.

If you are a westernized Chinese person reading this, I strongly urge you not to do away with this tea ceremony, no matter how modern you are. This tradition has its roots in feng shui symbolism, and it will do you good to follow it.

Drinking tea symbolizes eternal wakefulness. These are attributes that bring good fortune, according to a story that derives from an old tale involving Tat Mo, the Indian Brahmin generally credited with bringing Buddhism to China. He is said to have been the originator of the tea plant. Legend has it that one day he fell asleep while meditating. When he awoke he was determined that this would never happen again, so he cut off his eyelids. These fell to earth, took root and became the first tea plant. This is why, the elders say, drinking tea keeps you alert and awake!

Peonies bring romantic happiness 126

The beautiful peony is an excellent symbol for love and romance. It signifies beauty, passion and the amorous sentiments of youthful lovers. This flower comes in a variety of stunning colours, but the pinkish-red version is the one most associated with young love, and usually the one that is most valued. A painting of pink and red peonies in your home signifies that you have young single daughters who are eligible for marriage.

Displaying peonies in the living room always benefits the family's daughters. They are said to bring many suitors with honourable intentions, wit and charm.

Chinese folklore contains many stories about the peony. Some say the legendary figure, known as the White Peony was the pseudonym of a fairy creature so skilled in the arts of love that she became a legend among those who pursued such pleasures. The beauty and love-making skills of the famous concubine Yang Kuei Fei was also likened to the peony. Legend has it that she decorated her living quarters profusely with the mountain peony and that this encouraged the Emperor's desire for her to continue unabated – the peonies acted like a love potion!

The peony, however, is not always a good symbol to use. Displaying peonies in the bedroom is an enticement for a sexual (and sometimes illicit) entanglement. I always discourage couples, particularly those who have been together for a decade or more, not to hang a painting of the mountain peony in their bedroom as it can activate the man's libido so excessively that he looks for "sweet young things" outside the marriage.

A peony painting or vase of peonies should always be placed in the living room. This is for a family's young daughters and any young, single people staying with the family. Once they're married, remove the painting.

How to win back a loved one 127

Those of you who are suffering from depression or unhappiness, due to estrangement from someone you love, may wish to try this suggestion from a feng shui practitioner in Europe, who assured me that it is a most effective technique for winning back a loved one. It is supposed to be an excellent way of making up with someone with whom you have quarrelled, or had a severe misunderstanding. This technique will supposedly restore the status quo that existed before the big fight. I share this method with you because it was given to me by someone with the right kind of motivation, and I have used it once or twice. It worked, although I must confess that the misunderstandings I used it to clear away were small. Nevertheless, you may wish to try it.

How to resolve an argument

You will need four portrait-size rectangular mirrors.

- Take a portrait photograph of yourself, preferably a picture that shows you looking happy and smiling. Stick it onto the back of one of the mirrors.

- Then take a picture of the spouse, friend or person with whom you argued and wish to make up with. Again, use a picture in which the person is smiling. Stick the picture onto the back of another mirror.

- Take the last two mirrors and stick them together back-to-back, with the mirror surfaces facing outwards. Now place the pictures on either side of the centre mirrors so that they are facing each other, only with the two mirror surfaces in the centre. Tie together with red thread.

- Leave them together like this for seven days and nights, then call the person with whom you have argued. You will be surprised by the cordial reception you will get. From then on, it will be up to you.

128

Kitchens and storerooms in the south-west can harm relationship luck

Try not to have storerooms and kitchens in the south-west part of your home. If a kitchen is placed in the south-west, it creates afflictions for all the relationships of a house's residents. If your kitchen is located there and you can't do anything about it, try at least to make sure that your sink and refrigerator are not in its south-west corner. In order to alleviate difficulties caused by this unhelpful location, it is important to keep the kitchen well-lit.

If a storeroom is sited in the south-west, the problem becomes more severe as all the relationship luck of the home's inhabitants will be kept locked in darkness in the storeroom. However, the smaller the storeroom is, the less of a problem it represents. The solution to this affliction is to keep the room adjacent to the storeroom, and the storeroom itself, well-lit. At the same time, do not keep brooms, mops and other cleaning tools inside this room as this could cause your relationship luck to be severely afflicted.

129

Avoid two mattresses on a double bed

Married couples should never sleep on two separate mattresses placed on a double bed frame. This creates the chi of separation and is sure to lead to eventual separation, and even to divorce.

This taboo should still be observed even if a double bedspread is used and the two mattresses are well-camouflaged. The hidden split separating the mattresses creates serious rifts and unhappiness between the two people at a very deep level. Even though it may not be apparent at first, when the couple's differences ripen, their parting generally will be very ugly.

It is far better to have separate twin beds since this creates two focus points of chi which define the existence of the separate entities composing the couple. The beds need not be placed beside each other.

I have often been asked for the solution to husbands and wives having different KUA numbers and, hence, different auspicious sleeping directions. One way to accommodate this difference is to use twin beds that can then be moved to accommodate each partner's lucky direction. Do not worry about any slightly awkward arrangements that result. Just make sure that both parties have their beds placed against a solid wall.

In the case of more mature couples, it is not a bad idea to even have different rooms as this maximizes auspicious chi for both. With favourable chi, even though the couple may be sleeping in separate bedrooms, they will grow closer and be happier with each other than when one party is sleeping in a bad direction.

Marital beds also benefit greatly from a round headboard, since this creates symbolic support and protection for the sleeping couple. In fact, beds with no headboards lack this support and should therefore be avoided.

Love and Flying Star feng shui until 2004

Flying Star feng shui is is an advanced formula of compass school feng shui which reveals the influence of time on the feng shui forces that affect your home. One of the energies that changes over time is the chi energy that affects family and marriage luck.

How Flying Star works

Flying Star feng shui uses a special natal chart of the home. This chart reflects the period during which a home was built or was last extensively renovated (this establishes the ruling period number) and the direction that your main front door faces.

We are living in the period of 7, which runs from 1984 until February, 2004. After that date, we will be in the period of 8. Feng shui experts maintain that the number 7 stands for current prosperity, while the number 8 stands for future prosperity. Each period lasts for twenty years, so the period of 8 will last from 2004 to 2023, after which the period of 9 will begin.

In Flying Star feng shui, the direction in which your main front door faces establishes your home's orientation. (According to the Flying Star formula, there are a total of 24 possible door directions, each of which is said to occupy a sector of 15 degrees on the compass – practitioners of Flying Star therefore need to take directions very carefully.)

However, you do not have to understand Flying Star feng shui to benefit from it – I have extracted the essence of Flying Star recommendations for you in the following pages. The

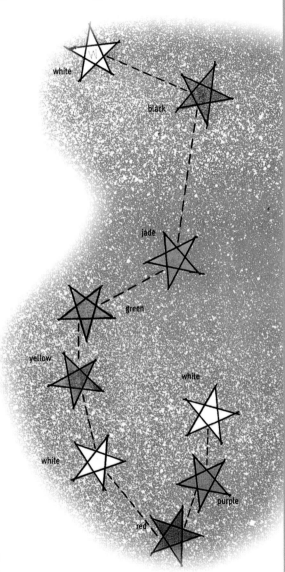

Above: The nine stars of the sickle are the basis of Flying Star feng shui.

charts included show the important areas in your home for love, marriage and family luck Bear in mind that this analysis is based only on houses and apartments that were built or last renovated between 1984 and the present day.

131   Flying Star natal charts

The Flying Star chi of the present period of 7 is represented in the Lo Shu grid reproduced here. Note that the number 7 is in the centre, because this represents the current period (1984–2004). According to Flying Star, the luckiest sector for love is the corner that has the star 4 (here in the south-west) and the star 1 together (here in the north-east). During the period of 7 the main star number 4 is located in the south-west, which symbolizes the powerful luck of relationships, while the main star 1 is located in the north-east, also a sector with powerful earth luck. This means that in the period of 7, anyone with bedrooms located in the south-west and north-east of their home enjoys excellent potential for marriage luck.

Lucky love areas

To pinpoint the areas in your home that will be lucky for love until 2004, look up your door direction grid in the following pages and see which sectors have the small numbers 4 and 1 – these have been specially highlighted, because they represent where these "star" numbers will have "flown" – these are summarized in the table on the right. For example, we can see that the year 2002 is very good for love and romance if you energize, sleep in or face the south-west and north-east directions. The south-west is especially lucky, so you must make certain that this area of your home is not afflicted with a water feature. This could lead to the negative side of love luck taking hold, resulting in scandals and unhappiness instead of joy and happiness. So, remember to keep the south-west clear of the water element.

What the numbers mean

When studying the natal chart of your home, the small numbers are more important than the big number in the centre. The small numbers define the water and mountain stars, which offer clues about the exact nature of chi energy in the eight corners of the home. The star to the left of the big numeral is the mountain star, and the one to the right is known as the water star.

To check the Flying Star chi of your house photocopy the grid relevant to your house's door alignment. The Lo Shu square should then be superimposed onto the house space, and the numbers in the grids used to analyze the quality and attributes of the chi that is present in each of the nine different compass sectors of the home.

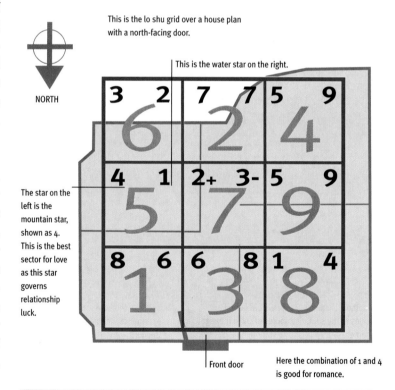

NORTH

This is the lo shu grid over a house plan with a north-facing door.

This is the water star on the right.

The star on the left is the mountain star, shown as 4. This is the best sector for love as this star governs relationship luck.

Front door

Here the combination of 1 and 4 is good for romance.

Flying Star chi for the period of 7

YEAR	The "4" is in:	The "1" is in:	Luck of marriage and love is:
2000	South	North-west	Average in both sectors
2001	North	West	Average in both sectors
2002	South-west	North-east	Excellent in both sectors
2003	East	South	Very bad in both sectors

The love luck of homes with north-facing doors

The natal chart (A) is that of a house with a north-facing-door. This is a door that faces the area between 337.5 and 352.5 degrees, the first sub-sector of the direction of north. When studying the natal charts of houses, the small numbers are more important than the big number in the centre. These small numbers define the water and mountain stars, which offer subtle clues about the exact nature of chi in the eight corners of the home. The star on the left is the mountain star, and the one on the right is the water star.

Note that in this natal chart, the two sectors that have the little 4 and 1 stars are in the east and north-west sectors. If your house is like this, then these are the sectors which hold out the promise of excellent romance and marriage luck.

So, based on Flying Star theory, you may wish to move into bedrooms located in either of these two sectors. If you cannot

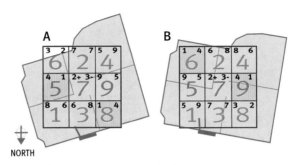

NORTH

sleep here, you may want to energize the areas to enhance your love luck further.

For the eastern sector, place a plant in full bloom there. This will activate the mountain star.

In the north-west sector, place a metal wind chime with six rods to enhance its water star. In a house like this, rooms to avoid for bedrooms are the west and south-west.

The natal chart (B) applies to houses also facing north, but the direction of the front

door is facing the second and third sub-sectors of north, i.e., between 352.5 and 022.5 degrees. This is generally a lucky house but, in this period, the two stars, 4 and 1, have moved to different sectors. Maximum love luck has also flown to the west and the south-east.

So to harness love luck, consider sleeping in either of these two sectors. Otherwise, magnify your love luck by placing a flowering plant in the south-east. Fresh flowers here also attract good love luck. In the west, place a bright light to energize the mountain star. A bright light also symbolizes warmth, which will cause the wood element of the number four to bear flowers and fruit. The rooms to avoid for bedrooms are those in the east and north-east.

The love luck of homes with south-facing doors

The natal chart (A) is that of a house with a south-facing-door. This is a door that faces the area between 157.5 and 172.5 degrees, the first sub-sector of south. When analyzing the Flying Star natal charts of houses, we analyze the small numbers, which represent the water and mountain stars. In this method, these star numerals offer excellent clues to the subtle attributes of chi in the eight corners of the home. The star on the left is the mountain star, while that on the right is the water star.

Note that in this natal chart, the two sectors that have the little 4 and 1 stars are in the east and north-west. If your house is like this, then these are the sectors which are promising for good romance and marriage luck. Therefore, based on Flying Star theory, you may wish to move into a bedroom located in one of them.

If you cannot sleep here, you can energize them to enhance your love luck.

Place a metal wind chime in the eastern sector to enhance its water star. Do not use water to activate this star, as it will cause problems. Instead, use a four-rod wind chime tol activate the water star. In the north-west sector of the house, place a mountain painting to enhance the mountain star. In a house set in the north-west, the bedrooms to avoid are

those in the west and south-west.

The natal chart (B) applies to houses also facing south, but here the front door faces the second and third sub-sectors of south, i.e., between 172.5 and 202.5 degrees. Here, the two small stars, 4 and 1, have moved to different sectors; maximum love luck has flown to the west and south-east. To harness love luck, you should sleep in either of these two sectors. Otherwise, magnify your home's love luck by enhancing the mountain star in the south-east and the water star in the west. In the south-east, place a flowering tree in a large clay container. Do not place water here to activate the water star, as this will harm the mountain star. In the west, place a seven-rod wind chime to energize the water star. In this house, the rooms to avoid are those in the east (very afflicted) and north-east.

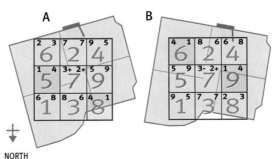

NORTH

134 The love luck of homes with east-facing doors

The natal chart (A) is that of a house with an east-facing door. This is a door that faces between 067.5 and 082.5 degrees, the first sub-sector of east. When analyzing the Flying Star natal charts of houses, we analyze the small numbers, which are said to be the water and mountain stars. In this method of feng shui, these star numerals indicate the more subtle attributes of chi in the eight corners of the home. On the left is the mountain star, while on the right is the water star. Note that, in this natal chart, the two sectors that have the little 4 star do not have the 1 star. So the love luck in this house is not very pronounced. However, the south-east has the 8 and 4 combination, which is auspicious. The south, with the 4 and 9 combination, is

also good. Bedrooms located in either of these sectors will enjoy good, although not excellent, love luck. Unlike the houses facing north and south, the love luck here has no potential for negative or dangerous energies. Those wishing to energize the water star in the south-east can use water, but this will jeopardize the mountain star, so I recommend that this place be kept free of energizers. In the southern sector, place a bright light to

enhance its mountain star. This will bring exceptionally good luck. In this house, there are no rooms that are particularly bad.

The natal chart (B) applies to houses also facing east, but the front door faces the second and third sub-sectors of east, i.e., between 082.5 and 112.5 degrees. In this house, the stars 4 and 1 also do not occur together, but the combinations 4/9 and 8/4 have moved to different sectors – to the north and north-west respectively. These sectors are auspicious, although marriage luck is only average. It is, however, possible to activate the mountain star of the north and the water star of the north-west to improve the luck of marriage and romance in this house. In the northern sector, activate the mountain star with a big, healthy plant. In the north-west, place a six-rod wind chime to energize the water star. This house has no unlucky rooms.

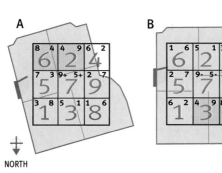

A

B

NORTH

135 The love luck of homes with west-facing doors

The natal chart (A) is that of a house with a west-facing door. This is a door that faces between 247.5 and 262.5 degrees, the first sub-sector of the western direction. An analysis of the Flying Star natal charts of houses focuses on the small numbers, which are said to be the water and mountain stars. These star numerals indicate subtle attributes of chi in the eight corners of the home. The little number on the left is the mountain star, while that on the right is the water star. Note that, in this natal chart, the two sectors with the little star 4 do not have the 1 star. This indicates that love and romance are not important attributes of the luck of this house.

However, the south-east has the 4 and 8 combination, which is auspicious. The southern one with the 9 and 4 combination also indicates good luck. Bedrooms in either of these two sectors will enjoy average love luck. However, unlike houses facing north and south, the love luck here has no potential for negative

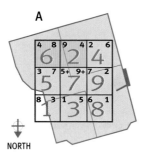

A

NORTH

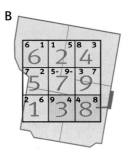

B

and dangerous energies. To energize the mountain star in the south-east do not use water, as this jeopardizes the mountain star, but instead, place a big, healthy tree here. For the southern sector, place a nine-rod wind chime there to enhance the water star; this will bring exceptionally good luck. In this house, there are no rooms that are very unlucky.

The natal chart (B) applies to houses also

facing west, but whose front door faces the second and third sub-sectors of west, i.e., between 262.5 and 292.5 degrees. In this house, stars 4 and 1 also do not occur together, but 9/4 and 4/8 have moved to the north and north-west respectively. These are auspicious sectors, although marriage luck is not especially pronounced in them. You can activate the water star of the north and the mountain star of the north-west for better marriage and romance luck in this house. In the north, water would be good, but might afflict the lucky 9 mountain star, so leave this area alone. In the north-west, set a large crystal to energize the mountain star there. This house has no unlucky rooms.

The love luck of homes with north-west-facing doors 136

The natal chart (A) is that of a house with a north-west-facing door. This is a door that faces between 292.5 and 307.5 degrees, the first sub-sector of north-west. An analysis of the Flying Star natal charts of houses focuses on the small numbers, which are said to be the water and mountain stars. These star numerals indicate subtle attributes of chi in the eight corners/sectors of the home; these are shown by the little star numerals. The little number on the left is the mountain star, while that on the right is the water star. Note that, in this natal chart, the two sectors that have the little star 4 are not combined with the 1 star. This indicates that love and romance luck is not great in this house. The southern direction

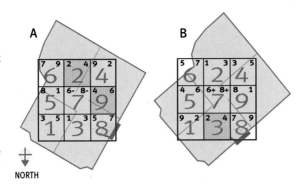

NORTH

has a 2 and 4 combination, which does not indicate good luck. The numeral 2 indicates an afflicted mountain star, which harms love luck.

A five-rod wind chime should be hung in the south to overcome the bad mountain star, and water should be placed here for the same reason. Water enhances the water star 4, and increases love luck. Also, the western sector

has a 4 mountain star which can be magnified with crystals. Having a bedroom in the west brings love luck into a house.

The natal chart (B) applies to houses facing north-west, with the front door facing the second and third sub-sectors of north-west, i.e., between 307.5 and 337.5 degrees. Here, the mountain star 4 combines with an auspicious 6 water star in the east. These numbers indicate that it is best not to place energizers here. Meanwhile, in the northern sector, the mountain star has the inauspicious 2, which makes it afflicted. Here hang a five-rod wind chime to control the mountain star and enhance the auspicious water star.

All houses facing north-west do not have severely unlucky rooms. The only troublesome room is in the north-east here, and in the south-west in house (A).

The love luck of homes with south-west-facing doors 137

The natal chart (A) is that of a house with a south-west-facing door. This is a door that faces between 202.5 and 217.5 degrees, and is regarded as facing the first sub-sector of the south-west. An analysis of houses' Flying Star natal charts focuses on the small numbers, which are said to be the water and mountain stars. These star numerals indicate subtle attributes of chi in the eight corners or sectors of the home; these are shown by the little star numerals. The little number on the left is the mountain star while that on the right is the water star. Love luck (both its negative and positive aspects) is said to be strongly indicated when the little star numerals indicate a 4/1 combination. In this natal chart the two sectors that have the

4/1 combination are the north-east and centre grids.

This indicates that the luck of love and romance is especially pronounced in these two sectors. The north-east has excellent love luck. Having a bedroom here indicates plenty of romance, which can be further enhanced by placing lots of crystals here. The centre of the house should be left well alone. Avoid having a bedroom in either the south-east or the

south, as these two sectors are afflicted. The west and north-west also have quarrelsome stars, so these too should be avoided.

The natal chart (B) applies to houses also facing south-west, but the direction of the front door is facing the second and third sub-sectors of south-west, i.e., between 217.5 and 247.5 degrees. In this house, the auspicious 4/1 combination has flown to the south-west; anyone who has a bedroom here will enjoy many romantic opportunities. To energize this area further, you can also place crystals here, but on no account should there be water. If you set water in the south-west, romance luck turns to scandals and bad luck. Avoid having bedrooms in the north and north-west, and also avoid disturbing the east and the south-east.

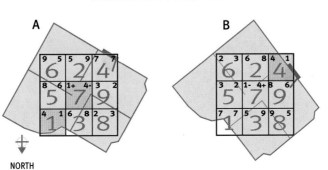

NORTH

138 The love luck of homes with north-east-facing doors

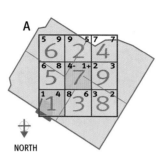

NORTH

The natal chart (A) is that of a house with a north-east-facing door. This is a door that faces between 022.5 and 037.5 degrees, the first sub-sector of north-east. An analysis of the Flying Star natal charts of houses focuses on the small numbers, which are said to be the water and mountain stars. These star numerals indicate subtle attributes of chi in the eight corners of the home; these are shown by the little star numerals. The little number on the left is the mountain star, while that on the right is the water star. Love luck (both its negative and positive aspects) is said to be strongly indicated when the little star numerals indicate a 4/1 combination.

In this natal chart, the two sectors that have the 4/1 combination are the north-east and centre grids. This indicates that the luck of love and romance is pronounced here. The north-east has good love luck. Having a bedroom in this area brings much romance, which can be enhanced by placing a wind

chime here. The centre of the house should be left well alone. Avoid having a bedroom in either the south-east or the south, as these two sectors are afflicted. The west and north-west also contain quarrelsome stars, so these also should be avoided.

The natal chart (B) applies to houses also facing north-east, but with the front door facing the second and third sub-sectors of north-east, i.e., between 037.5 and 067.5 degrees. Here,

the auspicious 1/4 combination has flown to the south-west, so a bedroom here is good for romance.

This combination of stars and elements indicates that the house cannot be enhanced any more, so do not energize. Do not place water here, either, as water in the south-west spoils romance luck. Avoid bedrooms in the north and north-west, and disturbing the east and south-east.

139 The love luck of homes with south-east-facing doors

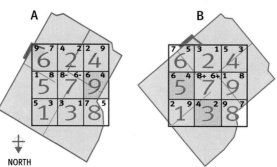

NORTH

The natal chart (A) is that of a house with a south-east-facing door. This is a door which faces between 112.5 and 127.5 degrees, the first sub-sector of south-east. An analysis of houses' Flying Star natal charts focuses on the small numbers, which are said to be the water and mountain stars. These star numerals indicate subtle attributes of chi in the eight corners of the home; these are shown by the little star numerals. The little number on the left is the mountain star while that on the right is the water star. Love luck (both its negative and positive aspects) are said to be strongly indicated when the little star numerals indicate a 4/1 combination. In the natal chart here, none of the sectors show this combination. There is a 4/2 combination indicated in the southern sector. This indicates a romantic

mountain star combined with an afflicted water star. It is best to leave this sector alone. Also, it is not a good idea to have the bedroom here. The best room to occupy for those wanting marriage luck is the one located in the west, which benefits from a 6/4 combination. This can be further enhanced by hanging a seven-rod wind chime there.

The natal chart (B) applies to houses

also facing south-east, whose front doors face the second and third sub-sectors of south-east, i.e., between 127.5 and 157.5 degrees. Here, the auspicious 1/4 combination is also missing, and the lucky 6/4 combination has flown to the east. So anyone who wants marriage luck should sleep in the east, which cannot be enhanced any more.

In this house, the room in the north is said to have marriage and romance luck afflicted by the water star numeral 2, which brings illness. It is best not to sleep in the north if you want the luck of romance. You can strengthen the mountain star and weaken the afflicted water star by planting a big tree in the north. Do not place a water feature here (even though it is in the north), if you want good romance luck. Do not harm the mountain star. If you do, then love luck transforms into sex scandals and heartbreak.

Changing your luck for the period of 8

One of the concerns facing Flying Star exponents these days, as we get closer to the year 2004, is the dilemma of having to decide whether to recommend that the main doors of homes be changed to take account of the period change from 7 to 8 in the early part of 2004. Owners of homes whose main doors face the auspicious double 7 star directions will be forced to consider that, during the new period of 8, the number 7 will no longer be auspicious. Indeed, the number 7 will become very inauspicious as soon as the period changes. This is because the number 7 in Flying Star feng shui stands for violence, and if a main door with the double 7 remains unchanged, the chance of your suffering from armed robbery will be very likely.

This is only one of several matters to consider, but it is probably the most severe. Having said that, however, I have studied the natal charts of the period of 8, and I can tell you that in those charts there are more unlucky than lucky sectors in homes. Some of this period's charts for certain door directions are so unlucky that there are only one or two "good" sectors in the home.

Master Yap Cheng Hai and I have, therefore, come to the conclusion that if you wish to make any changes to your door or house,

your renovations should start any time between now and the year 2004. This ensures that, although the period will have changed, your house will still remain a period of 7 house.

When you change your door direction, all you need to do is move or tilt your door very slightly so that, if it faces the first sub-sector now, it will face your second sub-sector, and vice versa. Then study the next four pages and take care that when you do your renovations, you do not inadvertently cause bad luck to occur by offending the Grand Duke Jupiter, the Three Killings and the Five Yellow. It is important to decide the timing of your renovation according to where these colourful taboos reside in each year. These are covered in the next few pages. You will find it rather tough planning your house renovations, and, if you really cannot help going against these taboos, the solution is to start work from a sector that is not affected by them during the year in which you undertake renovations. Remember that when you have bad luck due to bad feng shui, your relationship luck automatically suffers.

Below: If you need to change your door direction, plan your work carefully so that you do not cause other offences that could affect your relationship.

Doors with "77"
Anyone whose main doors currently enjoy the double 7 must change them. This affects houses with the following door directions:
North-facing door, facing 2nd/3rd sub-sectors
South-facing door, facing 1st sub-sector
South-west-facing door, facing 1st sub-sector
North-east-facing door, facing 2nd/3rd sub-sectors

141 Sectors for good relationships for the next ten years

Based on an analysis of the Lo Shu grids for the next ten years, from the year 2000 to 2010, the sectors of any house that will enjoy the best relationship luck in any year can be revealed. Once again, this method of feng shui is based on Flying Star feng shui, which explains the time transformations of feng shui luck. It is for this reason that Flying Star feng shui is regarded as the divining arm of compass formula feng shui. Flying Star enables practitioners to fine-tune their recommendations, since it can identify exact dates, and even times, when bad or good luck will occur. I have always felt that, so long as I know what the good and bad years are, I will be satisfied.

Flying Star assigns certain meanings to each of the numbers, which can be strengthened or weakened in accordance with the other star numerals that affect the sectors of homes based on their natal charts. What is presented here is not natal charts but Lo Shu square numbers that apply to different years. From these numbers, I can create the grid of numbers that applies to the year. Since there are nine grids, please note that these generalizations about lucky sectors repeat themselves every nine years. Fine-tuning occurs when you then compare the numbers of these charts' sectors with those of your house's natal chart (given in the preceding pages). Find the natal chart according to your main door direction.

Above: Crystals can be used to energize the most favourable love sector according to the Lo Shu grids from the year 2000.

Best relationship areas

Year	Lo Shu #	Luckiest love sector	Energizers to use
2000	9	South, North-west	Lights for the South, windchimes for north-west
2001	8	North, West	Wind chimes for both
2002	7	South-west, North-east	Crystals for both
2003	6	East, South	Lights for both
2004	5	South-east, North	Lights for the South-east, chimes for North
2005	4	Centre, South-west	Crystals
2006	3	North-west, East	Wind chimes for the North-east, lights for East
2007	2	West, South-east	Wind chimes for the West, lights in the East
2008	1	North-east, centre	Crystals
2009	9	South, North-west	Lights for the South, wind chimes for North-west
2010	8	North, West	Wind chimes for both

Paying respects to the Grand Duke Jupiter 142

In Flying Star feng shui, there is a very important gentleman who is regarded as the Deity of the Year. We call him the Grand Duke Jupiter, or Tai Tsui in Chinese, and it is important to know where he resides each year so that you can make very certain that you do not "offend him". There are also specific guidelines on how your can improve your feng shui if you are able to garner the support and assistance of the Grand Duke. Remember that you should never incur the wrath of the Grand Duke.

To find out what the Grand Duke's location is each year, refer to the table that is shown on the right.

The Grand Duke's direction

In the year of the:	The Chinese lunar years :			Grand Duke Jupiter is located in:
RAT		2008	2020	NORTH
OX	2009	2021		NORTH-NORTH-EAST
TIGER	2010	2022		EAST-NORTH-EAST
RABBIT	1999	2011	2023	EAST
DRAGON	2000	2012	2024	EAST-SOUTH-EAST
SNAKE	2001	2013	2025	SOUTH-SOUTH-EAST
HORSE	2002	2014	2026	SOUTH
SHEEP	2003	2015	2027	SOUTH-SOUTH-WEST
MONKEY	2004	2016	2028	WEST-SOUTH-WEST
ROOSTER	2005	2017	2029	WEST
DOG	2006	2018	2030	WEST-NORTH-WEST
BOAR	2007	2019	2031	NORTH-NORTH-WEST

Never confront the Grand Duke 143

Always remember that you must never confront the Grand Duke Jupiter. Therefore, each year always check where the Grand Duke is, and, in that year, make sure that you do not sit facing this direction when you are out on a date, writing a letter (or e-mail) to a loved one, or having dinner with anyone important. Instead, sit with the Grand Duke's direction behind you so that you obtain his support in whatever you are doing. The Grand Duke's patronage is very potent, and, even when his location is your best direction based on the KUA formula, you must not sit there in the year when it corresponds to the Grand Duke's direction. Note that in the year 2000 – the year of the Dragon – the Grand Duke is located in the east-south-east. In that year, anyone born during the year of the Dog clashes with the Grand Duke. The best bet is for Dog year people to lie low.

In addition, please also note that you should not dig or do any renovation work where the Grand Duke is. Finally, try to keep the sector quiet. Too much noise here offends him!

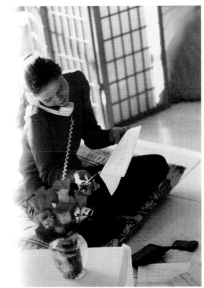

Above: Check the direction of the Grand Duke (see chart above) and make sure that you never sit facing him in your home, office or when you are out.

144

Confronting the Three Killings

Another important Flying Star factor to take note of is the Three Killings. The table below shows you where the Three Killings, or Sarm Saat, is located each year. Please note that, unlike the Grand Duke, this harmful feature occupies the four cardinal directions of the compass. So, while the Grand Duke occupies and affects only 15 degrees, the Sarm Saat occupies 45 degrees. Note from the table that in 1999 it occupies the west and that in 2000 it occupies the south.

The guidelines on how to handle the Three Killings are completely different from those for the Grand Duke Jupiter. Here is a summary of what you can and cannot do:

You must never have the Sarm Saat, or Three Killings, behind you in any year. So, in 2000 (the year of the Dragon), you must not sit with its direction – south – behind you. This means that you should not sit facing north. You

Above: The location of the Three Killings each year (see chart) should be considered. Never sit with it situated behind you.

may, however, face the Three Killings directly. This means that you can sit facing south. Confronting the Three Killings will not harm you, but having it behind you will. In the year of the Snake in 2001, the Three Killings is in the east, so in that year, the first millenium year, you must not sit with the east behind you. It is far more advantageous to sit directly facing east, thereby facing the Three Killings head-on. Remember this rule when you are out on an important date with someone whom you want to impress.

When you are planning to do house repairs and renovations, you must not do it in sectors that house the Three Killings. Thus, in 2000, this means you should not undertake any renovations in the southern sector of your house. You may, however, do so in sectors that are opposite the Three Killings.

Please note that, at all times, you must follow both these and the Grand Duke guidelines. They are necessary precautions to take when renovating your home.

Locating the Three Killings

Year starting February 4th:	THREE KILLINGS is in the:	In the years of the following animals:	Three Killings location is:
1999	WEST	OX, ROOSTER, SNAKE	EAST
2000	SOUTH		
2001	EAST		
2002	NORTH	BOAR, RABBIT, SHEEP	WEST
2003	WEST		
2004	SOUTH	MONKEY, RAT, DRAGON	SOUTH
2005	EAST		
2006	NORTH		
2007	WEST	DOG, HORSE, TIGER	NORTH
2008	SOUTH		

Avoiding the danger of the Five Yellow

There is a third direction that you should check every year – the one which signifies the place of the very deadly Five Yellow. This is the source of many problems, mainly related to accidents and illness, but also heartbreak and a great deal of unhappiness. It creates huge obstacles which block relationship luck. Like the preceding taboos, the location of the Five Yellow moves around and changes annually. Since it causes so many problems, it must be forcefully countered every year.

The best way to counter the bad luck and misfortunes brought by the Five Yellow is to use a five-rod pagoda wind chime. The pagoda design adds potency to the wind chime. There should also be tiny bells on it to dissolve the Five Yellow's bad energy. Hang the chime outside rather than inside the house; if your house happens to face the direction of the Five Yellow, the chime's presence there should reduce its danger considerably. Otherwise, always try to use another door. Locations of the Five Yellows are summarized in the table on the right.

The main taboo regarding the Five Yellow is that you must not undertake any renovations where it is located. Thus, if you are planning to have a new kitchen and the Five Yellow is located in its site, it is best to postpone the renovation until the following year, when the Five Yellow has flown into another grid. In the lunar year 2000, the location of this harmful manifestation of bad

Left: To dissolve the bad luck of the Five Yellow, hang a five-rod wind chime, ideally in the design of a pagoda, outside.

The location of the Five Yellow over ten years

Year starting February 4th:	DEADLY FIVE YELLOW is in:
1999	SOUTH
2000	NORTH
2001	SOUTH-WEST
2002	EAST
2003	SOUTH-EAST
2004	CENTRE
2005	NORTH-WEST
2006	WEST
2007	NORTH-EAST
2008	SOUTH

energy is the north; this means also that the north is generally afflicted during the year.

Please note that if you are making massive renovations that involve your entire house, then the taboos on the negative energies – the Grand Duke, the Three Killings and the Five Yellow – no longer apply. But check that you do not start work in a direction which houses any of these three manifestations of bad energy.

Certainly if you want to energize marriage luck, do not sleep in rooms located in any of these three directions, either! By observing these Flying Star taboos, you will take account of time considerations in your feng shui practice, and strengthen your chances for success.

146

Send a wish for love into the universe on a balloon

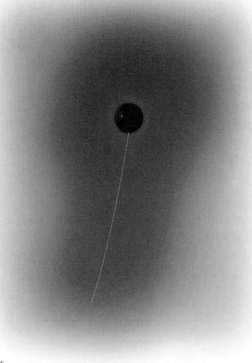

Here is a wonderful and fun way of attracting love into your life. Try it on a lazy Sunday morning when breezes blow and the sun is shining brightly. Buy yourself a few helium-filled balloons and take them to a park or any open ground where you know your balloons will be able to fly high into a cloudless sky and then disappear into the universe.

Choose balloons that are brightly coloured, and make sure that you have an assortment of colours – reds, yellows, whites, pinks and lavenders. Do not send aloft balloons that are blue, green or black. You want to release yang rather than yin energy.

Get a black felt-tip pin and compose your message of love carefully. You do not have much space to write on, so do make certain that you plan before you begin. Think through what you want to wish for. If you want someone to share your life with, make sure you throw in a few descriptive words. Don't leave things like that to chance. Consider what kind of partner you want. If looks are important to you, put in something that directly addresses physical appearance. If financial security is important, describe that too. Be specific. Remember that your goal is to send your wishes into the universe so that your environment will help to return them to you in a material form.

Above: Releasing bright, yang balloons with your wishes into the atmosphere can bring romance into your life.

Balloons of love

Put *one* wish on *one* balloon. This will focus the energy of the balloon on your *one* wish. When you have finished writing the words that best describe your heart's desire, release the balloon. Watch as it flies high into the sky. After it has attained some height, it will suddenly vanish. This is the moment when your wish has entered into the energy stream of the environment.

If you have several wishes, you should send *one* balloon up at a time. Organize a balloon-releasing party with your friends. After you have released all of your balloons, forget about the wishes you have sent into the skies. Let the winds and the waters bring about your wishes for you. You will be surprised how powerful this method is. Do not think excessively about the wishes you have made. By worrying about them, you will be sending forth negative vibrations that will create obstacles to your wishes being achieved.

My balloon wish made in 1986 was to be able to shop like an empress! The next year, I successfully acquired a chain of fashionable department stores and boutiques, and shopped like an empress for my stores for two years! Now I prefer to follow my lama's advice and release balloons with holy mantras written on them. Such balloons send blessings into the environment.

Blow bubbles in the wind on a day of the full moon

Another very enjoyable way of harnessing the energy of the wind is to send a full memorandum of requests and wishes to the benevolent God of Marriage who resides in the moon, from where he weaves matchmaking magic on the young and eligible men and women of the world. The God of Marriage is said to be an excellent energy source to tap if you wish to find a suitable partner or spouse who can make your life happy.

Night of the full moon

Choose an evening of the full moon. Check a Chinese calendar to make certain that you identify the evening correctly. It is only during the time of the full moon that "messages" can be successfully communicated to the God of Marriage. The best time to experiment with this wonderful ritual is the early evening when there is still some daylight in the sky. It is even better when there is a mild breeze, since you need the wind to send your wishes to the moon. The way you are going to communicate will be via bubbles, which are visualized to contain pictures of your wishes. So you will have to practise engaging your imagination and your mind. You must imagine yourself with the person you love beforehand. If you are not dating anyone currently, but want to get married and wish that someone suitable would come along, try picturing yourself on your wedding day. Visualize yourself dressed in all your finery and beaming with a big smile. Practise putting this image into a lavender or pink-coloured bubble.

Next, go to the toy department of any store and look for the best soap bubbles kit you can find. Then take your kit with you to a park, a playing field, or your just own garden. When you are relaxed, start blowing bubbles into the wind. Practise, and you will see that the bubbles are usually tinged with lavender or lilac.

Practise blowing really big bubbles; try to make them as large as possible. When you have perfected this, mentally picture yourself smiling and happy with your loved one inside a bubble. This picture can be of yourself with someone whom you are dating who is being coy about committing, or someone you admire – a vision of your perfect man or woman.

Visualize yourself and this person inside the bubble you are blowing, and then blow it into the universe. Imagine it flying to the moon to invoke the blessing of the God of Marriage. If you can't blow a perfect big bubble into the sky, it is not your time, but, if you can send forth many big bubbles, be prepared for a pleasant surprise!

Below: Blow perfect bubbles on the evening of a full moon and visualize yourself with a loved one to encourage marriage.

148

The 49-day signing ritual

The 49-day signing ritual was passed on to me by a famous feng shui master. He told me that one can achieve almost anything with this ritual if it is done correctly, but it must be done in conjunction with the prosperity signature. According to personalized feng shui, signatures that start and end with an upward stroke are believed to create growth, or sheng, energies which then attract good success luck.

To embark on this 49-day ritual, please note that this method requires everything to be written longhand in your own slow

Below: Write what you want from a love partner, new or existing, repeat 49 times, sign 49 times, then burn it. Do this ritual every day consistently for 49 days.

handwriting. You cannot have it typed or photocopied, since this completely destroys the magic of your own hand creating your own special energies.

First, gather your thoughts gently. Take several slow, deep breaths, watching them as they go in and out of your body. When you feel composed, write down exactly what you want in terms of love. Do you want your marriage to regain its former splendour? Do you want to find a husband to share your life with, a wife to start a family, someone to love you, a partner, a kindred spirit? Think through what you want very carefully and then write it down clearly. Try to be as brief yet as clear as you can. Remember, you must repeat what you write 49 times. You then have to sign the paper 49 times using your new prosperity auspicious signature.

When you have finished doing all that in one sitting, you are supposed to burn the sheets of paper. The next day, repeat this ritual again, and continue doing it for 49 days in a row. You must not skip any days. If you do, you must start all over again. If, halfway through the ritual, you decide that you no longer want what you wished for, just stop. If you wish to change what you wrote, then you will have to start the count all over again. Master Yap Cheng Hai told me that no one to whom he has given this method has ever succeeded in finishing the 49 days!

Hang love banners to catch the Dragon's breath 149

This is another ritual that taps into the magical wafting energies of the wind. Not many of us realize that the wind carries a million messages and signals that are sent forth by all the living creatures of the universe. The wind encapsulates all the chi – both good and bad – of our environment. When we release balloons and blow bubbles in the wind, we are riding on the good sheng chi of the winds. When winds blow gently, their chi is said to be benevolent. When they blow harshly, they contain killing energy (as during a hurricane). The Chinese use their colourful language to describe the energy of the winds as the Dragon's cosmic breath!

The practice of hanging banners high up to catch the wind, the breath of the Dragon, is based on the same principle. The best place to hang these banners are places that are as high in the air as possible. So, if you live on the upper floors of a multi-level apartment building, this is an excellent method for you to use.

Think of these banners as flags. Design them as beautifully as you can, with good fortune images that suggest love, romance and marriage for you, if that is what you want. Write on them the wish that will make you happy. Seriously consider what will make you really happy.

If you are feeling rather lonely, and want a more active social life, write a request for that on them and decorate your banners with lots of yang energy. This means using yang colours like red and yellow.

If what you wish is to have a soul mate or partner to love, include the double-happiness symbol on them. Then write down your wish for this to come about.

Energize your marriage

If your marriage is boring, and you feel your spouse is losing interest in you, wish for the energy between the two of you to sizzle once more. Draw symbols of undying love like pairs of geese or mandarin ducks on the banners.

If your sex life has become boring and you wish to re-energize it, draw lots of peonies on them. Then write down your wish for greater sexual bliss.

You can actually decorate your banner in any way you wish. When you are satisfied with it, hang it from your bedroom window and let it catch the wind. The more it flutters in the wind, the more its positive energy is being sent out to actualize it all for you. If you live in a house, you can, hang it from your window.

Do not worry when the rain and sun eventually absorb the colours of your banner. Let it hang for at least seven days and nights before taking it down. Do not talk about it to anyone. Love rituals must never be talked about loosely, as you can send out negative energy without realizing it. If you can, burn the banner after use.

Above: to make your love wishes come true, write them on paper banners, decorate them prettily and hang them outside your bedroom window. The picture above shows prayer flags fluttering in the breeze, blessing the Dragon's breath of the surrounding environment.

150 Turn on the yang light for 49 nights

Perhaps the most powerful representation of yang energy is a very bright light. Lights of any kind belong to the fire element, which produces the earth energy so excellent for all kinds of relationship luck. Lights that are in a round shape are the best energizers.

I remember each time a young lady came to me to honestly confide her fervent wish to find someone with whom she could have a steady relationship, I would almost always suggest that she place a light in the south-west corner *or* in her personal nien yen corner (based on the KUA formula of Eight Mansions, see Tips 68 and 69). I have discovered that women with such a wish who faithfully installed the light, *and kept the lights turned on*, were those who succeeded in getting what they wished for – a boyfriend, and in many cases, a husband.

It is no use merely placing a lamp anywhere for whatever purpose. You must turn on the light.

Please also note there seems to be something rather significant about the number 49. According to many of the old classics, we are strongly advised to always be especially careful when we reach the age of 49 – as this is a major turning point in life. If one succumbs to an illness during the 49th year, for instance, it is believed to be extremely dangerous in that it will be long drawn-out and even fatal. So, the old folks are usually reluctant to tempt the fate of the gods and celebrate the youngsters' 49th birthdays! Then there is the signing of the prosperity signature for 49 times to attract auspicious chi to all our signatures after that – a potent formula! Similarly, the advice is to turn on the light for at least three hours for 49 nights.

151 Place Dragon and Phoenix symbols in your bedroom

In feng shui symbolism, the Dragon and Phoenix are the two most powerful representations of auspicious chi energy. These are the celestial creatures that signify the apex of good fortune. Alone, the Dragon and the Phoenix each stand for different things and are yang. The Dragon symbolizes success, courage, leadership and imperial luck. The Phoenix signifies wonderful new opportunities, recognition, and the luck of revival and renaissance. The Phoenix always appears when a country enjoys a time of growth and prosperity.

When the Dragon and Phoenix are placed together side-by-side, however, they signify the powerful union of yin and yang actualized in marital bliss. This joint symbol is thus extremely powerful for enhancing the feng shui of marriage happiness for couples who

are already married, especially those who are newly wed, and the feng shui of marriage opportunities for single and eligible people who are not yet married but want to be. This image speeds up the ripening of marriage karma.

It is therefore very auspicious to use Dragon and Phoenix images in your bedroom. Place them side-by-side, with the Dragon set to the left of the Phoenix. They can be displayed as wall hangings, embroidered bed spreads, or paintings. They can also be carved onto beds, bedroom cabinets and dressing tables.

Display plum blossoms and chrysanthemums

One of the most significant of good fortune symbols, believed to bring positive good luck for young girls, is flowers. Plum blossoms and chrysanthemums are regarded as being exceptionally lucky for young unmarried women, whose purity and beauty they symbolize. It is for this reason that plum blossoms and chrysanthemums are popular in households with unmarried daughters. Displaying these flowers fresh, or as images in paintings, signifies the good luck that will be enjoyed by the young daughters throughout the year.

Auspicious plum blossoms

Plum blossoms signify beauty and splendour even in the winter months. The plum blossom and fruit symbolize pure beauty in adversity and indicate longevity, since the flowers are able to bloom on leafless and apparently lifeless branches of the tree even up to an advanced age. Plum blossoms also signify marriage luck, and are very popular during the Lunar New Year. Many households display specially imported plum blossom stems abundant with pink and white flowers. Sometimes fake blooms are stuck on to simulate the abundant flowering of good luck chi.

Yellow chrysanthemums are considered to be auspicious either to display, grow or present as a gift to someone. Buddhists are particularly fond of using these flowers as offerings on altars, and, during the Lunar New Year, these are the most auspicious flowers to display. A profusion of yellow chrysanthemums in a long vase or porcelain urn conveys strong and powerful yang energy which instantly attracts good luck into the home. Chrysanthemums signify durability and endurance. So, love, success, commitments, luck – anything that you wish to last forever – may be augmented by displaying these beautiful autumn flowers. When combined with any longevity symbols such as pine, bamboo, the crane or the deer, the possibility for a long life is considerably strengthened. Chrysanthemums with plum blossoms suggests a life of ease from start to end.

Orchids signify perfection and are considered emblematic of the superior man. Orchids also symbolize good family luck and plenty of children. In any case, they are emblems of love and beauty, and are particularly auspicious to have around.

Magnolias are symbols of feminine beauty and sweetness. This kind of flower is second in popularity only to the peony for signifying a beautiful woman and marital happiness. In the old days of China, only emperors and members of the imperial family were allowed to cultivate the magnolia plant. Magnolias are superb for wedding bouquets because of their symbolic meaning, and because they are white in colour.

Right: Yellow crysanthemums are thought to be a wonderful gift to give to someone as they bring good luck.

153 Attracting marriage chi at New Year

The Chinese believe that the best time to energize marriage luck for the eligible young women of a household is during the fifteen days of the Lunar New Year celebrations. There are many different activities that are connected with this objective, the most prominent of which is the much-publicized one of throwing mandarin oranges into the sea on the fifteenth day of the New Year. The night of the fifteenth is the official end of the New Year celebrations. I remember when I was in my early teens, my mother used to take me to the seaside esplanade in Penang to watch finely dressed young girls stroll along the beach as they waited for midnight when they would cast their well-chosen oranges into the sea. My mother told me this would bring good husbands to them – husbands who would bring financial security to the girls and their families.

Then my mother told me about a less well-known practice – that of lighting candles and placing them near the vicinity of the front door to welcome indoors marriage chi. The candles were to be alight for fifteen days, throughout the New Year celebrations, until they ended on the fifteenth day. I was told that many families preferred to light red lanterns instead of candles, which they kept alight all through the fifteen days of the New Year.

Encouraging good marriage luck

Another very auspicious time to repeat this ritual is during the seventh day of the seventh lunar month. If you light candles or hang lanterns on this day, and offer them to the seven sisters of the heavenly God, it is believed that all the young women of a household will

Above: Lighting red lanterns and dedicating them to the seven sisters of the heavenly God on the seventh day of the seventh lunar month, is thought to bring about good marriage luck.

become prettier. They will have good marriage luck and also attract husbands who will look after them.

I feel that a great deal of this is based on superstition, but I have always had great respect for the beliefs of any community. I am convinced that, were one to look hard enough, there is always a sound basis for many of the practices that are said to cause good luck and chase away bad. Therefore, I share these particular practices passed on to me by my mother!

When I reached my teens, I performed these rituals, and successfully found a husband when I was barely twenty-one years old. Whether this was eventually good or bad luck is a matter of opinion, although I have to say that, while we may have had our ups and downs, my husband and I are still together after over thirty years of marriage.

Decorate with the double-happiness symbol 154

The double-happiness sign is so potent that, in addition to wearing it, you can also decorate your bedroom or home with it. In the Forbidden City, and in many of the old family mansions of wealthy and powerful families in Beijing, which I have visited, the double-happiness (and longevity) symbols are pictured everywhere.

In addition to seeing them on every decorative object and work of art – paintings, ceramics, urns, cloisonné ware, and so forth – what was most revealing to me was how many of the windows, balustrades and corridors, including the doors of the Forbidden City, had this symbol incorporated into their designs. It was the same story in the Chinese mansions. In particular, the double-happiness sign was freely used in the bedrooms of the emperor – ostensibly to create great marriage luck for the Son of Heaven.

It is, therefore, not a bad idea for those wishing to energize the luck of marriage to do the same. Look for beautiful objects that have double-happiness symbols drawn on them and place them either in the corner associated with love in the living room, or decorate the bedroom using this motif. Most important is to have this symbol carved onto tables, beds, cabinets and desks meant for the bedroom. You should never sleep or step on this symbol, since this indicates that the feng shui is being spoiled.

So do not have such symbols embroidered onto bed sheets or pillow cases. Never have them woven into carpets either.

Wearing the double-happiness symbol 155

The Chinese are great believers in symbolism and many are so familiar with the powerful good fortune symbols that you see them painted, embroidered, carved and drawn on almost all the decorative pieces of artwork for the home. Among the symbols of marriage luck, perhaps one of the most popular is the double-happiness symbol.

There are several different ways of harnessing the luck of this symbol, which also has several layers and nuances of meaning. For single people, the double-happiness sign brings the luck of marriage. However, modern single people have neither the inclination nor the belief to put this symbol in their rooms. I have therefore devised a way of wearing the double-happiness sign so that it stays with you all the time.

OE Design worked with me to create a small, exquisite collection of feng shui jewellery for modern people. One of the symbols I insisted on using was the double-happiness sign, and they have come up with a beautiful interpretation of it.

Those who are engaged and contemplating marriage should wear the double-happiness ring as a marriage ring. It will bring you continuous happiness in your marriage. Single women should wear double-happiness earrings. Worn high on the body, the chi created lifts marriage luck to the upper chakras. The symbols will bring wonderful marriage opportunities. Single men should wear double-happiness cufflinks or tie pin.

156 Women can use the Dragon's yang energy for love

Feng shui is very much about balance. The best way of invoking this balance is to try to have an instinctive understanding of the unique blend of forces that are at work when we deal with the Dragon image.

For women who wish to attract the intrinsic male chi into their orbit, they can use the symbolism of the Dragon very effectively. For this, the full frontal dragon will be the best representation to use, as this represents the image of the emperor.

I once purchased a gift of an imperial dragon image for a single girlfriend. She had been enormously successful in her career, but love seemed to have been indifferent to her – until I gave her a full frontal, five-clawed imperial dragon, which she hung in pride of place above her fireplace in the living room. It

Below: The Dragon is very powerful for boosting love luck when it is placed in the living room.

changed the energies of her living room, and her home, instantly, and made it come vibrantly alive with yang energy. She herself became happier as she responded to the new energy. Shortly thereafter, she found someone with whom to share her life. They got married and moved back to England, where the dragon continues to hang in their home in Holland Park.

A potent love symbol

The Dragon is especially potent for energizing love luck for single women who live alone or only with their mothers. The presence of all-yin female energy creates an imbalance. If the overall décor of the home also reflects this excessively yin theme, marriage luck does fly out of the window.

All that is needed to correct this is to harness the chi of the Dragon. The best place to create the yang presence is the living room. It is not a very good idea to put the Dragon in the bedroom, because here it becomes excessively yang. When a single girl places a dragon image in her bedroom, she will exude excessive quantities of yang energy and scare men off.

I have successfully brought love into the lives of fairly aggressive career women who had the dragon image in their bedrooms. Every time, soon after I removed the dragons, they each got engaged and married. All they needed to do was to move the dragon into the living room, for positive chi!

Men, energize the yang chi of the Phoenix

An excellent symbol for single men who may be looking for love and a suitable partner to marry, and with whom to start a family, is the heavenly Phoenix. These wonderful celestial creatures signify the feminine yin energy, but they are also very yang creatures. This duality of the Phoenix symbol works very well for encouraging good marriage luck for single men.

Right: Images of the Phoenix or other birds such as the peacock can be placed in the living room to bring romance to bachelors.

Boosting yang for marriage

Men also need to activate yang energy if they wish to get married and need some feng shui luck to find a suitable mate, but to use a dragon would create an inauspicious imbalance. Even for those engaged in a homosexual relationship, having two dragons could create imbalance. Men should use the Phoenix to find love in the same way that women should use the Dragon. Men are the hunters in any relationship situation, and the Phoenix will bring many opportunities for the single man to find love.

As with the Dragon in the case of single women, once again, it is not a good idea to place the Phoenix in the bedroom. It is much better to have a painting of the Phoenix in the living room. Bachelors will find that this instantly brings new energy into a home. Please note that the Phoenix does not just bring love luck. The Phoenix also creates other auspicious vibrations which permeate a home. Residents will always enjoy new avenues opening up for them so that they may constantly move forward to better things.

If you cannot find a suitable Phoenix image, using a colourful full-plumaged bird like the rooster or the peacock will do just as well.

158   The lucky number eight

The number eight is one of the luckiest in feng shui terms – the powerful Pa Kua that has been used for centuries to map out homes has eight sides. The sectors of the Pa Kua that link to areas of your life – the aspirations – again are eight in number. It is considered a universally lucky number. Phonetically in Chinese it sounds like "growth with prosperity". In connection with encouraging love into your life, you can follow the eight most important ways, summarized

Left: Paired images such as doves can be very potent symbols in your love corner.

Eight ways to energize the love corner

1. Put red lanterns in this area.
2. Include red and yellow candles to bring in yang energy.
3. Place some paired images here, such as unpainted mandarin ducks or pairs of doves.
4. Put a clear quartz crystal here.
5. Use the double happiness symbol on its own or with lanterns.
6. Hang mountain pictures to support earth energy.
7. Use the lover's mystic knot as a feature on furniture and carpets.
8. Display narcissus and peonies.

Above: Red candles boost energy in your south-west area.

below, to energize your relationship sectors in the south-west of your bedroom and living room. The bedroom needs to be right for successful relationships, so make sure you follow the eight tips below to make your love life flow freely and happily.

Eight tips for the bedroom

1. Sleep in your nien yen direction.
2. Place the bed diagonally opposite door.
3. Always have a rounded, solid headboard for support.
4. Hang a picture of a loving couple.
5. Remove or cover up all mirrors facing the bed.
6. Do not have water features such as aquariums in the bedroom.
7. Do not sleep under exposed overhead beams.
8. Keep computers and televisions out of the bedroom.

Finding the man of your dreams

If you have been a single female or male for some time or are searching for a new fulfilling relationship, you can create this reality by focusing on what you want out of your new love match. You should list what you want out of your new partner and put it in your south-west corner in your bedroom, energizing it with light and paired objects. The universe is quite happy to send you the partner that you want, but you have to be very specific about your needs and desires. If you list too many frivolous qualities you will get someone who may be fun to be with short-term, but who will eventually break your heart because they are not truly committed to the relationship. Or if you list too many worthy attributes you may find the partner that comes to you ultimately bores you because they are so serious that they are no fun to be with.

Also be sure to list whether you want a heterosexual partner, if that is your preference, or you may find a wonderful, caring lover who turns out to be gay.

Making your wish list

To find your ideal partner, list all the qualities you would like in your future lover on the left-hand side of a sheet of paper. Think carefully about what characteristics you put down, as your desires will normally be realized. Think about this partner as your soul mate and the person you want to spend your future life with. On the right-hand side, list the less attractive qualities that you would be willing to tolerate – there always has to be balance in every partner. For a man, he might tolerate a woman who goes out dancing and gossiping with her friends. With a woman, she might be willing to put up with a man who regularly goes out drinking with his friends and occasionally goes to football matches

When you have carefully considered your list and finalized it, write it out again neatly and then put it in a small gift box, tie it with red ribbon to give it some yang energy, and then place it in the south-west corner of your bedroom and wait for the universe to do the rest of the searching work for you. Don't keep adding to your list as this will cause confusion; you will do better to spend more time compiling the list in the first place.

Below: It is possible to find your ideal soul mate, and making a list of what you want from your ideal partner can help you focus on the best partner for you.

The mystic knot to symbolize endless love

Left: The mystic knot is a lucky symbol for love that is often represented on furniture, furnishings and ornaments.

The mystic knot is a Chinese symbol for endless love. It represents a long life uninterrupted by separations, heartbreak, illness, setbacks or suffering – obviously an unnatural state, but nevertheless the ultimate aspiration of lovers. It is also known as a lucky knot and as an emblem it is extremely popular. Today you will find it being attached to other good luck symbols such as coins and amulets. The endless knot is also embroidered onto tunics and jackets, and carved onto furniture, woven into carpets, and painted on screens and porcelain ware.

Its significance in feng shui is as an easy-to-use motif that can be incorporated into the design and pattern of grills, doors and furniture. It is a symbol for longevity and endless togetherness. It also signifies good health. But it is most widely used as the perfect emblem for undying love, thus it has also been identified as a lucky love symbol suitable for ensuring that the romance in a marriage will last. It is therefore an excellent motif that can be carved onto beds and other types of bedroom furniture, and incorporated into window grid designs.

There is also a spiritual meaning to the endless knot, in that it stands for "no beginning and no end" – reflecting the Buddhist philosophy that existence is one endless round of birth and rebirth – a state the Buddhists refer to as samsara. The knot is therefore a wonderful reminder that once we realize this great noble truth about existence, we will want freedom from the endless cycle of births and rebirths – this samsara. This symbol is also on the breast of the Hindu deity Vishnu, and it is one of the eight signs on the soles of Buddha's feet.

It is an excellent idea for lovers to wear the mystic knot.

The cowrie shell for love while travelling

The conch, or cowrie shell, shown below right, is a symbol of auspicious luck while travelling. In olden times, the shell was an insignia of royalty and those in the employ of royalty would benefit from carrying a shell or having the shell symbol worked into their tunics. This was said to give them protection.

From a feng shui perspective, the shell can be used to attract business and relationship luck from overseas. It holds out the promise of good contacts made while travelling.

The shell is an excellent symbol for those whose work and livelihood require them to be able to get along well with people and who particularly benefit from being well known, famous and respected. To create the luck of good name and good reputation, place a large marine specimen (about 15–20cm [6–8in] long or wide) of this shell in the southern sector of your living room. The cowrie shell can also be placed in the north-east and south-west to strengthen the energy of these areas. Strong energy in the north-east creates excellent education luck, while strong energy in the south-west enhances and improves relationship luck.

If you and your loved one live apart and you have a commuting relationship, place a specimen of this shell in the south-west corner of your bedroom, or in your nien yen direction. This will bring you opportunities for being together and create circumstances for your relationship to blossom. It is a good idea, in any case, to always have this symbol around, since it enhances your communication luck. People will understand you better and your interaction with friends and colleagues will be most cordial and pleasant.

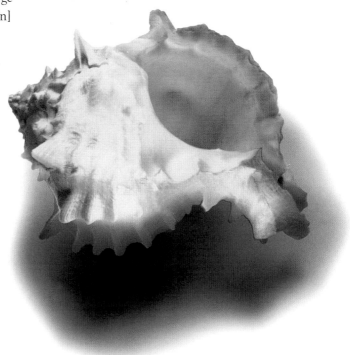

The cowrie shell

Right: If you have a long-distance relationship, place a cowrie shell in the south-west corner of your bedroom or nien yen direction. This symbol will help create more time for you and your partner to spend together, and encourage the relationship to be more rewarding for both of you.

162 The double-fish for abundant bliss

In feng shui, the fish has absolutely wonderful symbolism – it stands for abundance, wealth, harmony and connubial bliss. When shown as a pair, the fish symbol does not merely signify happiness doubled. It also denotes the joys of physical union between lovers and spouses.

It is, therefore, an exceptionally good symbol to display around the home of a newly married couple, or in the bedroom of young lovers. It brings great good luck for those in love, and it brings prosperity luck as well. Indeed, the double-fish is probably one of the luckiest symbols in feng shui practice. It is also considered to be one of the eight auspicious Buddhist objects, although from a Buddhist perspective, the double-fish symbol is viewed more as something of an amulet. In many countries of the East where there is a noticeably large Chinese population, the double-fish is usually worn as a pendant. It is also kept in the wallet as a powerful charm which is said to protect the wearer from being cheated and evil spirits, and helps to avert accidents. Those wearing the double-fish will

also not succumb to epidemics or others' bad intentions. In Thailand, a Buddhist country, the double-fish symbol is elaborately fashioned in 24-carat gold and worn by children from rich families for protection. Very often, these fish amulets have been blessed by monks and strengthened with additional amulets written on gold foil which are kept in the belly of the fish symbols.

Good karma with fish

One of the most wonderful Buddhist practices – said to generate enormous karmic merit – is the liberation of living creatures, and liberating the fish brings particularly great good luck. So when you free fish meant to be eaten, it is a very good deed. If you cannot do this, you can perhaps consider stopping the practice of eating live fish in restaurants, i.e., fish still alive and swimming. Having a fish killed specially for you to eat is the antithesis of fish liberation. If you eat fish that has already been killed, however, you are said to be eating a carcass, and therefore no negative karma is created by it. It is for this reason that I have given up eating steamed fish! Not only does it bring me bad luck, it also creates negative karma.

Left: The fish symbol represents abundance, money and harmony, and when depicted as a pair – married bliss.

The lotus for purity in love

The lotus is a stunning symbol of purity and perfection. For the Chinese, the lotus also has very spiritual and religious connotations. Its petals are said to symbolize the doctrine of Buddha's teachings. Buddha himself is usually depicted seated on a sacred lotus. His posture – with a straight back and lower limbs folded in front – is called the lotus posture.

Buddhist monks and holy masters all assume this posture when they meditate and teach the sutras. Dharma students also sit in the lotus posture when meditating or taking teachings. Those unused to this cramped position of the lower limbs are usually advised to practise sitting like this, as this is the posture most conducive to generating body quiet, thereby aiding the meditation process. A straight back is also said to encourage the chi flow within the body.

The mantra of the Compassionate Buddha – *Om Mani Peh Meh Hone* – is the lotus mantra and reciting it many thousands of times is said to bring a rain of blessings. The Chinese manifestation of the Compassionate Buddha is the Goddess of Mercy, Kuan Yin, and this mantra is, therefore, the Kuan Yin mantra. In Japan, this buddha is known as Canon, and in India as Avalokiteshvara. In Tibetan Buddhism, the Compassionate Buddha is known as Chenresig.

This great reverence and love for the lotus flower in the East stems from the importance of this symbol in many of the Buddhist traditions. In feng shui, the lotus is said to express the purity of love. Romantics who believe in and want old-fashioned love, which is not sullied by infidelity, but instead leads to marriage and a good family life, would benefit from incorporating the lotus symbol into their immediate surroundings. Bedrooms and living rooms that are decorated with the lotus plant or flower – real or artificial – will nurture a feeling of true peace and contentment.

Below: The lotus flower is a wonderful symbol that represents a perfect and very pure love.

164 The canopy or umbrella for protection

Left: A beautifully decorated umbrella placed outside the front door is thought to protect the home against intruders.

The canopy has the significance and meaning of protection – a covering and shelter from the elements much like the umbrella. The canopy can also symbolize the imperial umbrella, a token of someone held in the highest respect. It is an emblem of dignity and high rank.

So, we can say that, in a way, the canopy or umbrella represents victory and success in life's aspirations, which can be in one's career, in love and in the building of a family.

The umbrella is also a symbol of protection from negative influences. One belief is that the placement of an umbrella just outside the front door protects a house from burglars and from strangers with ill intentions. Umbrellas made of silk, decorated with tassels and painted with auspicious signs, when placed on the terrace of houses, are said to afford good protection. Such umbrellas should be placed in a diagonal direction, and never directly in front of, a house's main door.

In Thailand, the art of umbrella-making has reached great heights. Exquisite umbrellas made of bamboo and paper can be purchased in the northern Chinese city of Chiang Mai. They make good decorations and are excellent positive symbols.

Umbrellas also feature in wedding rituals. It is believed that, when a man marries, a silk umbrella should be held over his head as he walks towards his bride. This will ensure that after marriage he will gain high rank and honour. This is because usually only very high dignitaries and important people have umbrellas held over them.

Meanwhile, another umbrella ritual said to be very lucky and protective is when one is held over a woman in labour, as it ensures the safe delivery of her child. This can be a symbolic ritual utilizing a silk umbrella.

The vase for romantic happiness

The vase is a symbol of peace and harmony, and the placement of flowers in a vase, depending what kind of flowers they are, give rise to a plethora of rich symbolic meanings. As one of the eight auspicious objects, the vase symbolizes a receptacle for collecting good fortune chi – manifested in the form of peace of mind and happiness. In love, the vase symbolizes happiness in romance.

From a feng shui perspective, a large vase has several uses. If it is used to contain flowers, then it is a good thing to place flowers from the four seasons in it. Any combination whatsoever will create peace all year round for a household. These flowers need not be real. They can be made of silk – peonies for summer, chrysanthemums for autumn, orchids for winter and plum blossoms for spring.

A vase containing one stalk each of pine and bamboo, and placed in the centre of the home, or in its south-west corner, signifies that a couple will have a long and peaceful married life filled with a great deal of children luck. It symbolizes that the family as a unit will endure.

Filled with three symbolic halberds (a combined spear and battleaxe), it means successfully (and peacefully) climbing the career ladder. The vase can also be transformed into a wealth vase when filled with special precious objects. Vases that contain auspicious

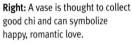

Flowers for good feng shui

Good fortune flowers can be selected on the basis of their colour:

- Red-tone flowers for the south. Carnations, red roses, gerberas, tulips, chrysanthemums
- Blue and violet flowers for the north. Bluebells, violets, irises, lavender
- White flowers for the west. Lilies, white roses, daisies, orchids, magnolia
- Yellow for the south-west and north-east. Buttercups, sunflowers, gerberas, daffodils

- Peonies, chrysanthemums, orchids and plum blossoms can be used for peace.
- Pine and bamboo can be used for children luck.

symbols can be placed anywhere in the house except the kitchen. Also, fresh flowers should not be placed in bedrooms.

When you purchase Chinese vases and urns, it is wise to be careful that you do not purchase the variety that is used for keeping the ashes and bones of ancestors. It is better to buy modern crystal or porcelain vases that also serve to enhance the earth element of the south-west corner or central grid of the home.

Right: A vase is thought to collect good chi and can symbolize happy, romantic love.

166

The sacred wheel for wisdom in love

Above: The Tibetan Buddhist Wheel, showing the six realms of samsaric existence drawn in. This image is believed to bring protection to households when hung near the vicinity of the front door.

The sacred wheel is one of the auspicious signs believed to be on the soles of Buddha's feet. It is variously referred to as the Wheel of Life, the Wheel of Truth, the Wheel of a Thousand Spokes, and the Wheel of the Cosmos. It symbolizes the noble and "wisdom truths" of Buddha's teachings. Some say the wheel symbolizes the Buddha himself. The turning of the wheel represents Buddha's doctrines, or Dharma, being taught by lineage teachers, called gurus or lamas.

From a feng shui perspective, the wheel represents the inner feng shui of the mind. The wheel signifies overcoming the three poisons of existence. These three poisons are ignorance, anger and attachment – considered to be the three root causes of human suffering. The wheel thus symbolizes the conquest of suffering by overcoming the three poison arrows that cause suffering for human beings!

Placing the wheel symbol in the house signifies gaining peace of mind and growing in wisdom. It is particularly suitable for those looking for a soul mate who can bring happiness to their love relationship. The wheel thus enhances the wisdom aspects in finding love. An image of a wheel would benefit those seeking love, if it is placed in the north-east of the bedroom.

The north-east also relates to the earth element. Placing a wheel there will ensure that even if you are in love, you will stay well grounded, and that wisdom will prevail in your selection of a life-long mate. The wheel is said to bring the luck of wisdom. It is, therefore, an excellent symbol to have around for those who are contemplating marriage or starting married life together. The wheel creates also the chi of harmony and tolerance.

The good luck jar – for all your good fortune

I have been told that not many genuine feng shui masters like to reveal too many of their secret practices. One of these secrets, which they keep silent about and which is considered to be an integral part of their feng shui practice, is that it is important to keep a jar for symbolically storing good fortune. So, to make the practice of feng shui complete, households should display what is known as the good fortune jar. A receptacle with a cover is meant to symbolically "lock in" all of the good fortune that is being activated by the good feng shui of a well-arranged house. The jar then becomes the household's auspicious jar. I have noticed that in master Yap Cheng Hai's house, he has many jars like this in every room, all filled with special goodies such as semi-precious stones and red packets filled with good luck money.

In this connection, I must add that master Yap's house is also very cluttered, but I can assure one and all that he enjoys extremely good feng shui. So, although I like to live in a neat and orderly home, and I love the good energy of a well-organized space, I have to say that clutter does not necessarily bring bad feng shui. I also deem it absurd to pay a feng shui "consultant" lots of money merely to tell you to keep your house tidy!

A precious jar

I also want to say that, personally, I do not view the jar as a feng shui energizer in the sense of it bringing any additional material advantage or benefit. I regard the jar as a precious and auspicious object because I see many references to it in many of my Buddhist texts. In Buddhism, the jar is for containing precious

Left: When you choose your wealth jar, select one with dragon or bat images. To energize for romance, choose mandarin duck or flying geese images.

holy relics of buddhas and revered lamas, which are considered significant good fortune to have in the house. But this is not feng shui.

Placing a jar like this in the house is therefore not necessarily a feng shui recommendation unless it is used as a "wealth jar". Used this way, aside from the connotations given above, the jar can also be a receptacle for containing the symbolic wealth of a household. In this way, you can treat it like a wealth jar, filling it with semi-precious stones, pretend gold bars, old coins and other precious things; cover and keep it hidden away in your bedroom.

If you plan to have such a wealth jar, it is a good idea to choose one with auspicious designs drawn on it. Dragon and bat images are excellent for this purpose. Those wanting to activate love and marriage should select a jar decorated with mandarin ducks or flying geese.

Using all eight symbols for protection

Shown here are the eight auspicious objects which, when combined together into a single symbol, offer protection against misfortunes of all kinds, including those of love and marriage. It will ward off people who are untrustworthy and whose intentions towards you are negative and dishonourable.

These eight objects are regarded by Buddhists as being exceptionally good when displayed together. Their presence is believed to bring complete good fortune to a household – the kind that addresses not only the material luck of the family, but also the spiritual luck that brings peace of mind and real happiness.

In fact, many Buddhist households display banners and wall hangings that have these eight objects printed or sewn onto them to promote good luck.

As a feng shui tool, wall hangings that have these eight objects make excellent antidotes for overcoming the bad feng shui of doors being placed one after another in a straight line. Used this way, a wall hanging becomes a door curtain which transforms fast-moving shar chi, or "killing breath", by slowing it down so that it then turns auspicious. Where a room divider of some kind is required, you can also use wall hangings embroidered with these eight objects.

So, if your door is too close to a staircase, for example, using a door hanging with the eight auspicious objects on it would overcome any bad chi present. These eight symbols can be displayed collectively as paintings or drawings on walls, or as eight separate objects. I recommend that you have these symbols in your home to welcome the good sheng chi into it and to create protective energy around your house so that the love that has arrived continues to grow, and love that has yet to come will come in a way that will bring real happiness.

The eight auspicious objects

When the eight auspicious are combined together they give the people displaying them protection against mishaps and any problems in relationships and marriage.

lotus flower

canopy

vase

good luck jar

double fish

cowrie shell

mystic knot

sacred wheel

Above and left: The eight auspicious objects work best when displayed as one symbol as they protect the house and the owner's marriage.

Picture Credits

The publishers are grateful to the following for permission to reproduce photographs:

Abode UK: tips 9 above, 13, 37 left, 57 below

AKG, London/Erich Lessing: tip 53

John Bouchier/Elizabeth Whiting Associates: tip 16 above

Britstock-IFA: tips 11, 34, 42, 57 above, 61 above, 74, 159, 163

Nick Carter/Elizabeth Whiting Associates: tip 60

Christie's Images, London: tips 40, 61 below, 81 below, 83, 86, 87 below, 90, 93 above, 95, 97 above and below, 98 below, 99 left, 100, 102, 103 above and below, 151, 157 left and right, 160, 162, 167 above and below, 168 and back cover

Geoff Dann: tips 2, 15, 26, 49, 65, 117, 153 and pages 6 above right, 7 below right

Michael Dunne/Elizabeth Whiting Associates: tip 62

Andreas V. Einsiedel/Elizabeth Whiting Associates: tip 31 below

Neal Farris/Photonica: tip 120

Fitzwilliam Museum, Cambridge: tip 113 and front cover centre left

Gonkar Gyatso/Tibet Images: tip 166

Huntley Headworth/Elizabeth Whiting Associates: tip 14

Rodney Hyett/Elizabeth Whiting Associates: tips 12, 36 above, 141 and page 5 centre left

Image Bank: tips 28, 37 below right

Tim Imrie/Elizabeth Whiting Associates: tip 3

Lu Jeffrey/Elizabeth Whiting Associates: tip 6

Andrew Kolesnikow/Elizabeth Whiting Associates: tip 52 above

Hisanori Kondo/Photonica: Tip 161

Tom Leighton/Elizabeth Whiting Associates: tips 7 left, 44 and page 6 centre left

Di Lewis/Elizabeth Whiting Associates: tip 45

Mark Luscombe-Whyte/Elizabeth Whiting Associates: tip 5

Kaoru Mikami/Photonica: tip 152

Takeshi Nagao/Photonica: tips 33 below, 63 below

Phillips Fine Art Auctioneers, London: tip 39

Photodisk: tips 1, 27, 77, 112

T. Sawada/Photonica: tip 25 and page 5 below right

Wilhelm Scholz/Photonica: tip 118

Science Photo Library: tip 63 above and front cover centre right

Kenichi Seki/Photonica: tip 148

Sotheby's Oriental Department, London: tips 9 below, 36 below, 81 above, 85, 91, 93 below left, 94, 99 right, 101, 156, 158 above,165 and page 6 centre left

Tony Stone Images: tips 8, 10, 16 below, 17 above, 18, 19, 21, 22, 33 above, 51, 52, 59, 64, 66, 67, 68, 72, 79, 84, 92, 96, 98 above, 104, 114, 115, 121, 122, 123 above, 125, 143, 144, 147, 149, 158 below and pages 1, 5 above right and below left, 6 centre right and below right and front cover above and below left

Superstock: tips 31 above, 48

Telegraph Colour Library: tips 43, 88, 123 below, 124, 140

Lillian Too: tips 41, 155 and front cover below right

M. Toyoura/Photonica: tip 119

Victoria & Albert Museum Picture Library, London: tip 87 above

Neo Vision/Photonica; tip 17 below

Keiji Watanabe/Photonica: tip 164

Elizabeth Whiting Associates: tips 18 below, 20, 23, 71, 75

Linda Wrigglesworth Chinese Costume & Textiles, London: tips 7 right, 35, 38, 46 and page 5 above left

Kit Young/Garden Picture Library: tip 145

David Zaitz/Photonica: tip 146.